THE EYE OF THE HEART

ALSO BY HARRY W. PAIGE...

Songs of the Teton Sioux

Wade's Place

Night at Red Mesa

Johnny Stands

The Summer War

Shadow on the Sun

Tunes and Testaments (poetry)

Land of the Spotted Eagle:
    A Portrait of the Reservation Sioux

THE EYE OF THE HEART

Portraits of Passionate Spirituality

HARRY W. PAIGE

A Meyer-Stone Book

CROSSROAD • NEW YORK

1990

The Crossroad Publishing Company
370 Lexington Avenue, New York, NY 10017

© 1990 by Harry W. Paige

Cover design: Terry Dugan Design

Manufactured in the United States of America
94 93 92 91 90   5 4 3 2 1

Library of Congress Cataloging-in-Publication Data

Paige, Harry W., 1922–
 The eye of the heart : portraits of passionate spirituality / Harry
W. Paige.
  p.   cm.
  ISBN 0-940989-58-1
1. United States — Religion — 1960– 2. Spirituality — United States —
History — 20th century. 3. Paige, Harry W., 1922–   . I. Title.
BL2525.P35   1989
291.4'0973 — dc20   89-40243
                                                              CIP

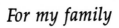

For my family

*All that is vital is irrational
and all that is rational is anti-vital,
for reason is essentially skeptical.*
—MIGUEL DE UNAMUNO—

CONTENTS

PREFACE

A SHAMAN-PRIEST OF THE SIOUX INDIANS who was a personal friend once told me that for America to realize its true destiny its people must learn to see with *ChaNte Ista*, the Eye of the Heart. He went on to explain that we must learn to see, not with the eyes alone but with the heart. And it must be a new way of seeing, of understanding leading to new perceptions, new visions. I remember him as a man of great insights, a man who always saw beneath the surface of things — one of those rare prophets of the prairie who had little formal education but who had lived intimately with *WakaNtaNka*, the Great Spirit, and who had learned what really matters.

My friend might have been describing the methods of science as well as religion, for science frequently requires new ways of seeing familiar things. From the discovery of gravity to the discovery of relativity or of "black holes" in the universe our scientists have been forced to see the natural world in new and different ways. And sometimes, as in the case of environmental concerns, the scientist must become humanist as well, taking into consideration the greater good as well as purely scientific objectives.

To see with *ChaNte Ista* requires faith, my friend explained — faith in God, the Great Spirit; faith in science

11

or art; faith in oneself or others; sometimes faith in the land itself. To do what Americans have done, to be what Americans have become, faith has had to be a partner in our trials and endeavors along the way.

The essays that follow are about faith and about seeing with *ChaNte Ista*, the Eye of the Heart, for my friend and my own experience have convinced me that they are a part of the same process. Most of the people portrayed are believers, those who have come to faith the hard way — through struggle, sacrifice, and prayer. Those who have made their own Stations along the way. They represent different ethnic groups, different age groups, different levels of spiritual intensity and insight. Some we may feel are guilty of excessive passion — like the Penitente Brotherhood of the mountains of northern New Mexico, who crucify one of their volunteer *Cristos* on Good Friday, or the old Mexican-American woman who made the Stations of the Cross on bleeding knees *outside* the church.

The essays are about memory too, for memory is what remains after experience ends. Some of the people in these pieces are the gentle tenders of memory, trying desperately and faithfully to keep alive a ghost church and the people who once worshipped there, a kind of private and perpetual All Souls' Day of the heart. Some are Native Americans of the Plains who seek their Lord in remote and dusty places like Wounded Knee and Spring Creek and who go off to lonely buttes to cry for a vision. Some even sacrifice their flesh at the ancient Sun Dance, now with its strong Christian overtones. Some are like people in our own towns, our own parishes. But Indian or white, Hispanic or Anglo, young or old — they are all truthseekers who have put their faith in *ChaNte Ista* and who have come to see ancient truths in a new light and who have chosen to live by those truths.

ACKNOWLEDGMENTS

ACKNOWLEDGMENT IS GRATEFULLY EXTENDED to the following for permission to include here essays originally published elsewhere:

America, for "Golgotha in New Mexico "(March 23, 1974); "A Death on the Prairie" (June 24, 1978); "Sacred Places" (January 21, 1989).

The Catholic Digest, copyright by the College of St. Thomas, for "Stations of the Cross" (published as "A Woman of the Cross," April 1989); "To Be a Pilgrim" (June 1977); "Ghost Church" (November 1988); "The Vision of Noah Jumping Eagle" (November 1986); "Without Memories We Are As the Wind" (May 1982); "Mass Here, Mass There" (September 1973); "Reflections on a Catholic Boyhood" (April 1973); "Jugglers, Bell Ringers, Exiles" (March 1982); "The Unbeliever in My Church" (July 1982).

To *The Westerners* (New York Posse, Brand Book), for "The Yuwipi Cult Among the Sioux" (vol. 19, no. 2, 1972).

GHOST TOWN IN NEW MEXICO

The slow and smokeless fires of decay light the
                    western sky
    where the pale adobe ruins, like dreams set out to dry
    hold hostages to memory.
Out behind the church the dead, held like a hand in
                    a game of chance,
    lean on the wind. Cloud shadows dance
    and waiting things seem almost free.
Hay balers, wagon wheels and arrowheads mix
                    their separate tales
    beneath a second-hand moon and then a sun that
                    again fails,
    even to wake eternity.

1.

GOLGOTHA
IN NEW MEXICO

IT IS GOOD FRIDAY OF THIS YEAR. Snow still drapes the purple heights of the Sangre de Cristo Mountains in northern New Mexico, a delicate mantle on shoulders of enduring rock. A strange procession winds its way through a pine-clad canyon that is clogged with drifts, the hard mirror crust reflecting the sun upward into the mountains. The Brothers of Jesus of Nazareth, a secret lay organization commonly known as the Penitentes, are moving toward *Calvario* to crucify one of their members, this year's volunteer *Cristo*, the imitator of Christ.

Rising above the whine of the wind are the mournful notes of the *pito*, a flute-like instrument whose sounds seem to lead the sad pilgrimage toward the New Mexican Golgotha, four miles away. Behind the flute player a man stumbles through the snow, dragging an eight-foot, two-hundred-pound cross behind him. A crown of thorns settles heavily on his brow, and blood tears run down his face and under the black mask he is wearing. His flowing robes, tied around the waist with a rope, cling to his back

17

where the crimson stains from a recent scourging cake the fabric in blood. Four men walk beside him — reviling him, spitting on him, and lashing him with whips of braided yucca soaked in water to make them heavier. Two men walk on either side of the *Cristo* carrying *santos*, ornate and artistic images of Christ and the Virgin.

Suddenly the *Cristo* falls for the first time on the *Via Crucis*, the Way of the Cross. He lies there on the frozen snow crust panting, his dark eyes glazed with pain and frantic from the ordeal he has been through. An old man with a white beard steps forward and gently helps the *Cristo* to his feet, speaking words of encouragement to him in his hour of suffering and sacrifice. Then, when the *Cristo* is standing, the old man wriggles himself under the heavy cross, straightening up with a groan and wincing with pain as the sharp wooden edges cut into his shoulders. Bowed under its weight, the old man drags the cross forward while the *Cristo* staggers beside him.

Following the *Cristo* and his fragile Simon are the flagellants, dressed only in baggy, blood-stained cotton drawers, their skins turned a gun-metal blue by the biting cold. On every third step they swing their cutting yucca whips over their shoulders and strike on one side of the backbone. Then three more steps and the whip falls on the other side. Between the rhythmic lashes they call out: *"Yo penitente pecador!"* "I, a repentant sinner!"

When the old man stumbles and falls beneath the cross, the *Cristo* takes it upon his own shoulders again and plods on. When he falls a second time a young woman, playing Veronica to his Christ, steps forward and wipes his masked face with her veil. The women weep and cry out as the Veronica holds up her veil to reveal the image of an anguished Christ drawn in blood.

At one of the crosses planted along the path to *Calvario* the procession halts to meet a group of black-shawled, barefooted women coming from the opposite direction. The women are members of the Order of Our Lady of Mount Carmel, and they carry a statue of the Virgin on a gilded pedestal. The women weep as they recite the rosary or sing hymns to the Mother of Christ. A teenage youth, who has been marching behind the *Cristo*, steps to the head of the procession bearing a large crucifix. Slowly the two figures are raised until they touch and appear to embrace. Both men and women prostrate themselves before the figures while the Passion of Our Lord is read. The ceremonial encounter is called *El Encuentro*, a symbolic and sorrowful meeting of Mother and Son on the *Via Dolorosa*.

The procession continues for an hour and, as the Brothers approach their *Calvario*, the *Cristo* falls heavily for the third time. There is an expectant hush as the people wait to see if he will rise again. The cross has cut deeply into his shoulders, and the wounds on his back have opened. He has left a trail of bloody footprints in the snow. The *Cristo* struggles to his feet and picks up his heavy burden again. Then he begins to stagger forward, moving slowly toward crucifixion's hill.

Finally the long and painful trek is over. The cross carried by the *Cristo* is thrown on the ground and he is bound to it with wet rawhide thongs — the arms at the shoulders, the legs at the thighs. As he is tied to the cross, the *Cristo* cries out: "Not with thongs! Nail me!" But, above his pleading, the cross is raised and set in its hole. The body of the *Cristo* quivers as his weight settles on his extended arms. The women gather around the foot of the cross, the loudest cries coming from the *Cristo*'s mother.

The *Hermano Mayor*, local leader of the Brotherhood, picks up a spear and pierces the side of the *Cristo*. Blood runs down the flesh, staining his garment, and the weeping of the women reaches a crescendo of grief. The *Hermano Mayor* then preaches a short sermon on the seven last words of Christ. After about twenty minutes the body on the cross goes limp, and the head drops forward. The circulation has been so impeded and the trip to *Calvario* so painfully exhausting that the *Cristo* has lost consciousness. Sometimes the crucified brother dies on the cross and, in so doing, the Brotherhood believes, assures himself and his family a place in the reign of heaven.

To the soprano crying of the women, the cross is lowered and the *Cristo's* limp and bloody body untied, to be carried back to the *morada*, the small adobe church and meeting place of the Penitentes. It is there, in the inner room of the *morada*, that the *Cristo* is nursed back to consciousness. Or it is there that his dead body is prepared for secret burial. A year later the grave will be marked by a large Penitente cross.

That night the ceremonies end with *Las Tinieblas*, meaning "darkness," commemorating the desertion by the apostles and the time when darkness descended on the face of the land, rocks split, the dead rose, and the temple veil was torn. One white candle, representing Christ, and twelve yellow ones, representing the apostles, burn on the altar, their flames dancing. As the twelve psalms are read, each of the yellow candles is extinguished in turn. As the white candle is hidden behind a black cloth, the room explodes in anguish and sound — wailing, stomping, screaming, the sounds of drums beating and heavy chains rattling. The pandemonium goes on for nearly an hour, after which time the black cloth is removed to reveal the white candle still burning brightly. The yellow candles are re-lighted, hymns are sung, and the villagers return to their mountain homes. But the Penitente Brothers remain until the

Sunday of Glory, when the joyful anticipation of Easter breaks through the Lenten gloom like a new dawn.

For most Catholics the preceding scenes may seem to be vestiges of medievalism resurrected in the remote mountains of the American Southwest — or an orgy of sadism, or violation of church law regarding "excessive penance." Some may regard the rites as an overly zealous application of Christ's directive: "Take up your cross and follow me." For a few, however, the Penitentes' Way of the Cross has the beauty and the passion of the world's greatest tragedy — the willing sacrifice of the Son of God for the sins of humankind. There is no greater theme, no greater drama. And yet, for many of us the darkness of Friday's noon is illuminated by the anticipation of an Easter dawn. We know the story has a happy ending, and so we are free to choose Easter's triumph over Friday's agony. And there is the danger that we may lose ourselves in Sunday's alleluias, deaf to the whisper from the cross.

The human mind is selective, and so are the cultures to which we belong. The Catholic experience in Spain has always chosen to emphasize the passion over the power. The tragedy over the triumph. Tears over *Te Deums*. The main symbol of Spanish Catholicism is the cross. And Spanish Catholics never forget it. Indeed, it may seem to the non-Spanish Catholic as though to them the joys of the Easter resurrection were but an anticlimax to the passion of Good Friday. Spain was also the birthplace of the great mystics of Catholicism — St. John of the Cross, St. Teresa of Avila, and others, many of whom advocated bodily penance.

In the New World the Spanish descendants of the conquistadors in the isolated mountains of New Mexico carried on their Old World traditions. Without priests or the authority of the church, after the Mexican and Pueblo revolts, the simple, pious mountain people went underground, establishing a lay authority that had evolved from the Third Order of St. Francis, an order that has come to be known as *Los Hermanos Penitentes*, the Penitent Brotherhood. Threatened by the encroaching Anglo culture, they developed their own folk religion, denounced finally by outsiders and the church alike. For years in the mid-nineteenth century they existed in a spiritual limbo, a time when the Brotherhood took over the duties of the church and continued to act as a social cement for this mountain pocket of resistance. Even under the bans of excommunication they continued their religious devotions, celebrating Mass within the protection of their isolated *moradas*. They ministered to the sick and buried the dead. They cared for the widows and orphans and perpetuated their Hispanic heritage in a hostile environment. For nearly a century the Brotherhood was synonymous with the Catholic church in the Spanish towns of New Mexico's north.

Today, *Los Hermanos Penitentes* are back within the church, officially sanctioned by it. In a statement signed and dated January 28, 1947, Archbishop Edwin V. Byrne formally recognized the Penitentes as "a pious Catholic society" under the authority of the Catholic church. An annual meeting of the *Hermanos Mayores* and their representatives is addressed by the archbishop and other church officials. Thus the lost sheep of the Sangre de Cristo have been brought back within the fold.

But formal recognition by the Catholic church has not changed the basic attitudes of the Penitentes. They still believe in penance as the most direct path to salvation. I remember talking with an old man in the Penitente town of Cordova, a man I had every reason to believe was a Penitente himself. He denied membership in the Brotherhood, of course, as they all do. But I had seen the Seal of Obligation, the cross carved into his back, and the livid scars of numerous lashings as he worked in his fields, shirtless under the summer sun. I noticed too that, while talking with me in the shade of a piñon tree, he kept his hands clenched into tight fists.

"Why?" I asked him. "Why do the Penitentes inflict such suffering on themselves?" Even as I asked the question, I thought of the middle-class Catholicism I had known for most of my life — the rational, comfortable Catholicism where one made the Stations of the Cross symbolically, bloodlessly, following a painted Christ around the walls of the church. "Why?"

His eyes seemed to darken and turn sadder, stagnant pools of sorrow. Then he smiled a crooked smile, showing broken, tobacco-stained teeth. "Christ suffered and died for us," he replied. "And we are only men. Can we not do the same for him?"

I wasn't prepared for the simple truth of his answer or the directness of his question, and so I just nodded a silent amen to his words.

When I left him, I held out my hand. He unclenched his right fist, gave me a quick handshake and clenched it shut again. I pretended not to notice, but I am sure I turned pale — just as I am sure that an arctic chill came over me and something gripped my heart. For I had seen the satin glaze of a huge scar in the palm of his hand.

Back in my adopted New Mexican parish, while I examined myself before confession, the spade-shaped, scarred hand of a Spanish-American field worker intruded itself between me and my petty sins. It accused me of a greater sin than I would confess, a sin of omission — the lack of *passion*. And in my imagination I could hear a Lord's echo to the accusation: "Be ye hot or cold, but if ye be lukewarm I will spew thee out!"

The words, doubtless spoken by a sad and angry

Christ, ran through my mind even as I did my penance — five minutes of remembered prayer.

No, I do not advocate the harsh, bloody penance of
Los Hermanos Penitentes. And I realize that the faithful may suffer in different ways and offer that suffering
to Christ. But neither do I condemn the Penitentes, as
many do. For the redeeming factor in all their cruelty
and bloodshed is their passion. In a world that is often lukewarm to God, the Penitentes live at a spiritual
white heat. In a world that is secularly rationalistic, the
Penitentes can share a 2,000-year-old sorrow. In a world
in which the tragic sense has diminished, the Penitentes
can still feel — and weep. In a world in which the moral
sense is declining, the Penitentes can still see life as a
struggle between the forces of good and evil. In a world
that insists on togetherness, the Penitentes can go their
separate ways to Calvary. In a world in which the head
programs our lives, the Penitentes have chosen to follow
the heart. Over peace, they have chosen glory.

Few would deny that the practices of the Penitente
Brotherhood represent a penitential excess, a polarity of
passion. Yet such extremes can often serve to remind the
rest of us of what it means to "follow in His steps," as
St. Peter put it. The martyrs have helped show us, and
we have traced their bloody tracks through history. The
saints, too, have shown us the possibilities that exist for
sacrifice and perfection. They are the exceptions, those
who have demonstrated the human capacity to probe
the outer limits of faith.

A year from now, God willing, I shall probably be
back in my home parish in New York State. The mountains and deserts of New Mexico will belong to my past.
So, too, will *Los Hermanos Penitentes*, and the Brotherhood will seem as remote from twentieth-century eastern
America as Cervantes' Spain. But some Good Friday

afternoon as I keep an hour's vigil before a shrouded crucifix, I should not be surprised if a strange and lonely sound called me back to Las Truchas, Cordova, Questa, or Mora. Somewhere west of Imagination. A shrill, piping sound that tells of mountain places and rare mysteries in the thinner air where reason dare not follow. And for a few moments I shall follow the whine of the *pito* as it leads through snow-veiled canyons into the valley of passion. And I shall see a procession of half-naked, bloody men and sorrowing women threading its way toward a Golgotha of their own making.

Or perhaps an old man under a piñon tree will beckon me to step closer and put my finger into the scars in his hands and the place where the spear pierced his side. An old man who followed his Master, not wisely perhaps, but too well.

2.

STATIONS OF THE CROSS

I REMEMBER MAKING THE STATIONS OF THE CROSS, usually on Fridays during the Lenten season. It was a symbolic and bloodless pilgrimage around the inside of the church. But it was not a painless journey: even as a boy I noticed the faces of the people as they looked up at the images of innocent suffering, mirroring in their eyes the celebration of another passion almost two thousand years ago. I watched the old, arthritic limbs struggle to bend. I heard those limbs creaking in protest. And I remember wondering at the time why most of those who made the Stations were old and often infirm. It took me a while to learn the answer to that.

But on a Good Friday in the mountains of northern New Mexico I found a new meaning to the Passion at a place where symbol and fact seemed to meet suddenly and unexpectedly — like the sun and rain to form a rainbow of understanding.

I had been on the road, traveling around the winding, mountain roads of the north doing the necessary research on the Penitentes. It had been a difficult job with many frustrations and I had already made up my mind that this bizarre behavior of the Penitentes might represent an excess of passion in the latter half of the twentieth century. I was now all set to write a story mildly critical of the brotherhood.

I went around a hairpin turn, descended a few hundred feet into a valley where a town suddenly appeared as if by magic, framed by the snowy, sun-lit splendor of the mountains to the north and east. The highest structure in town was the church, its steeple and cross seeming to probe the clouds. I wound my way through the town with its washed-out, pastel adobes and its scattering of modest commercial buildings. A poor town, I thought, like most of the towns of the north. An isolated town as well. Yet somehow rich in faith, rich in belief. The poor and the faithful — they seemed to go together now as in biblical times, perhaps because the poor needed a faith so badly.

The church was a jewel in a rarer setting. It looked far too grand for the surrounding community but it also boasted quietly of priorities: we have put our wealth in God, it seemed to say. In things that rust and moth do not corrupt. In symbols of eternity. You have your symbols; let us have ours!

I decided to go in and share an hour or two of Christ's Passion with strangers who were not strangers. We shared something — these poor people from the mountains of northern New Mexico and the writer from northern New York. We shared a faith, a belief in the things of the spirit. We spoke different languages, worshipped in different communities; yet the bottom line was the same: we believed in the same God. And so I felt spiritually at ease, whatever the surroundings. Every church wore the furniture of home.

Suddenly I noticed I was not alone. A few pews ahead of me an old woman knelt in prayer. She had a square peasant's face and dark, glistening eyes. It was a face etched in a web of lines that seemed to go through and score the bones. Strangely, her hair was still coal black and shining as though Time had chiseled everything else away and left the crown untouched. The fall of her hair was pulled back tightly from her face until it disappeared beneath a black shawl that fell to her waist. The hands were stiff, gnarled and grasping as roots in flinty soil and the plain, black rosary beads that dangled from her stiff fingers seemed to have grown there like a vine.

She knelt leaning forward over her beads like a huge, black tear about to fall. Her beads dripped into the pew ahead of her as her fingers sorted them, drawing the dangling crucifix toward her an "Ave" at a time.

Suddenly, as I watched, she rose slowly, unfolding her limbs like something being uncovered in dark snow. Then she moved slowly, duck-like in canvas sneakers that made a squeaking sound on the floor. She walked around the stained-glass perimeter until she came to the First Station set in the wall beneath the Spanish words: "Jesus is condemned to death."

Drawing her squat body erect she bowed in adoration and chewed the soundless words of prayer. Before moving on to the Second Station she crossed herself with a graceful fluttering of the hand — the motion of a bird in flight. She passed under the warm glow of stained-glass saints balancing on a cloud and reaching out to birds and little children, aglow with innocence. When she left the Fourteenth Station on the opposite side of the church she shuffled to the rear, dipped her fingers in holy water, and made the Sign of the Cross in water beads. She genuflected stiffly, facing the pallid starkness of the stripped altar, an altar in mourning. Then she left. I looked at my watch — quarter to twelve. A few people began drifting in, mostly Mexican-Americans and Indians. A slant of sun coming in the window was making me drowsy. My head fell forward —

A voice broke in: "Can you help? She's bleeding."

I looked up at a woman, obviously a tourist, her face threaded in concern, almost in panic.

I looked at her, not understanding.

"An old woman," she went on. "She's going around the outside of the church on her knees. She's bleeding. I can't find the padre."

I got up and followed her outside where the same old woman was moving on her knees on the rough gravel and dirt, moving in the noontime sun toward the Fifth Station. The old woman's knees were scraped and bleeding. Her brown stockings were torn. Her face was set in a mask of stolid determination.

"She appears to be making the Stations — but on the outside of the church," the woman tourist whispered. "She's fallen once and I'm afraid..." She finished with a gesture.

I looked around for help and saw the padre just entering the church. The tourist woman and I hurried over to him and she explained what had happened.

The padre's expression did not change. He nodded solemnly. "I know all about it," he said through a Spanish accent and moved to pass into the church.

"She is quite old and she has fallen once," the tourist woman explained. "And her knees are bleeding."

The padre's face was expressionless, his voice soft and lyrical. "She is one of my parishioners. She has been making the Stations in this way for a long time, long before I came here. It's her way of sacrifice and penance. The people in the valley know it. Please, do not be alarmed. It is her way. A voice spoke to her when her son went off to war...."

"But, Father," the woman interrupted. "She has fallen...."

"God will not give her a cross that is too heavy," he said patiently. "Please, go on inside. Do not worry. There is nothing you can do. It is her way. Each of us follows the Lord in our own way. Which of us is to say which is the right one? And now, if you will excuse me."

And then he was gone, a dark shadow into shade.

"I can't bear to watch," the woman whispered and then followed the padre into the church. In a few minutes there was the sound of voices from within, a recitation in Spanish. It sounded solemn yet musical too — like something from another time.

The sweat was running down my face now and I noticed I was standing in the sun. At my feet was gravel and sand — abrasive as sandpaper. Yet she was moving on her knees to the next Station, dragging her legs behind her, two sticks in a coarse, brown wrapping. She moved no more than six inches at a time, throwing her knees forward and enough to the side to keep her balance. As she passed under the stained-glass windows she paused to raise the crucifix to her lips. Then she bent to prayer, her head bobbing slightly to her words. After a few moments she moved on toward the next stop on her journey.

I had an urge to go forward and help her to her feet, help her to the cool inside of the church. I wanted to explain to her that the Lord would accept her sacrifice if it were bloodless and made in the comfort of the church. He would even accept the prayerful journey if it were made from her pew, following Him only in her imagination.

But I did not speak her language. I do not mean the Spanish language but the language of suffering, of sacrifice, of penitence, of passion.

Suddenly she fell — and it was then that I moved forward to help her, feeling like a Simon two thousand years late. She looked up at me with darkly grateful eyes and then regained her composure and continued her journey. And it was at that moment that I knew the measure of my own faith! And it was then that I saw the Brotherhood of the Penitentes in a different light.

The language I did not understand was the language of passion. Peter in his denial and Thomas in his doubt had not understood either. It was only when Peter wept and Thomas found the hole in His side that they were made articulate, that they turned from head to heart.

Suddenly I felt utterly lost, as apart from Christ as any pagan in the world. I dropped to my knees and began following the old woman ahead of me. But I had only gone a few yards before I realized it was a futile gesture, a hollow gesture, a gesture as self-conscious as any I had ever made. Immediately I rose from the dust and gravel and directed my attention to the old woman. Her breathing was labored now but her eyes had a look of resignation, a look almost of peace as though something had been settled, some verdict passed. Some verdict I did not understand. I looked at the old woman, listened to the words coming from inside the church and I had the feeling that they were all speaking in tongues.

After a few minutes I turned from the old woman's painful pilgrimage and went inside the church. And there, for the first time, I prayed to understand a passion not my own.

3.

TO BE A PILGRIM

THE PROCESSION OF PILGRIMS winds up the mountain east of Las Cruces, "the place of the crosses," in New Mexico. The people have walked five miles from the Casa del Pueblo and the flat top of the mountain is in sight. A picture of Our Lady of Guadalupe is carried by the Second Captain at the head of the procession. The musical chanting of the rosary in Spanish is heard as the pilgrims stumble along the rocky trail.

The picture of Our Lady is a picture of the Dark Virgin, who appeared to Juan Diego in a place near what is now Mexico City in the sixteenth century. She is, the pilgrims claim, the patron saint of all the Americas.

The five hundred or so pilgrims are Tigua Indians, their Pueblo cousins, and Mexican-Americans. Only five are Anglos and two of them are there "on assignment," taking pictures or writing accounts of the pilgrimage. Most of the pilgrims are dressed for the December cold in jeans, heavy jackets, hats, and boots. One man wears an old Army jacket. A ragged army for Our Lady.

Two men and three women are barefoot. Later, on

top of the mountain, one of the captains tells me that the barefoot ones have a special sacrifice to make in gratitude to Our Lady of Guadalupe. In one case, a five-year-old daughter had a "hole in her heart"; the hole closed of itself. In another case a father recovered from a stroke. The word *miracle* is never mentioned; only the name of Our Lady.

One of the barefooted women is very old. Her dark, expressive face is furrowed and her wrists are like sticks poking from her black shawl. Her feet are swollen and bleeding from the sharp rocks and cactus thorns, and blue from the cold.

What sins, I wonder, does she atone for in this way? What barter for a soul in Purgatory? What promise made in passion or in prayer? I would never know, but somehow I was sure her intentions were for another. The greatest sacrifices are usually selfless.

The people rest from time to time, breathing in clouded gasps. But the chanting of the rosary goes on, as though independent of human breath, as though its prayers were carried on the chilly wind. Some of the men are carrying staffs as symbols of their authority. Others carry old automobile tires which they drop off at designated places along the way. Later, after dark, they will be burned to light the way down the mountain. Some gather dead yucca tops as they climb, to be carved into colorful crosses and designs called *quiotes*, used in the weaving of crowns.

From the top of the mountain the Mesilla Valley seems to flow west like a dusty sea. On a clear day you can see a hundred miles but today the sky is gray and wind-picked. Earlier in the morning snow had fallen; but it had stopped as the procession was about to begin, causing some of the pilgrims to whisper the name of Our Lady of Guadalupe.

The top of the mountain is dominated by two structures: an observatory belonging to the State University and a shrine to Our Lady belonging to the Tortugas pueblo community. At first glance the two seem incongruous, until one remembers that both are sighted on the stars and beyond. Science and religion, both sending out their signals, by light waves and prayer.

After placing the image of Our Lady behind the altar the pilgrims look for sheltered places in which to build their fires. They scatter all over the mountaintop, usually in kinship groups, and in a few minutes the smoke of a hundred fires is heavy on the wind. The people warm themselves, make coffee, and talk, waiting for the Mass to begin. Some go off by themselves to meditate and pray.

At eleven o'clock the Mass starts. It is said in Spanish, the music sung by a Mexican group in traditional costumes. At the blessing and consecration the people kneel in the sand and stones. Almost everyone receives Communion, walking through the parting crowd to the altar.

The old barefooted woman, leaning on a staff, limps painfully to receive the Host. Even the children are quiet as she passes, her black shawl spreading out behind her like a dark wake. What blessing she has earned from Our Lady is not known, but she has won the respect of the pilgrims.

After the Mass the people eat lunch and then make their *quiotes* from the yucca tops and the white underleaves. Most of them are fashioned in the shape of the Cross.

At four o'clock the women, wearing their handmade crowns, recite the rosary at the shrine, kneeling again in the sand and stones. The pilgrimage leaders proudly point out the numbers of young people participating in the celebration. The pilgrimage to Our Lady will continue for many years to come.

At dusk the women, the children, and the elderly begin the long descent, to wait at the bottom of the mountain for the men who will remain until after dark. It is a colorful procession: the *quiotes* seem to float on the dusk tide and the sound of the rosary is a whisper on the wind.

After dark the fires are lighted from the torches that the men will carry to light their way. They hold their *quiotes* high, following their leaders down the lighted trail, reciting the rosary as they go. To the city people beneath it is a breathtaking sight. The mountaintop seems to be on fire and the flickering torches draw blazing patterns in the night. When the men reach the bottom they join the waiting women for the long walk back to the Casa del Pueblo. The celebrations will continue there for another day and night.

As I walked along with the pilgrims toward the Casa del Pueblo I felt a curious elation, and at the same time a nagging disappointment. I had climbed the mountain with them. I had shared their food and drink. I had whittled my Cross of desert plants. I had attended Mass, offered up my private prayers. And I had come down from the mountaintop to the light of their fires. And yet I had the feeling that I was *with* them but not *of* them; that I was a spectator more than a pilgrim. That the meaning I took from that day on the mountain was not *their* meaning.

And it never could be. For I was a "head" Catholic, not a "heart" Catholic.

I found myself asking: "Lord, let me feel what they feel, if only for a moment." And I believe that has been the most constant prayer of my life.

I have witnessed it in others, this spiritual passion.

I have seen it in a church in Juarez, Mexico, on Good Friday. Just inside the altar railing, resting in a coffin, was a plaster effigy of a crucified Christ. And the people, weeping, wringing their hands, approached to touch it. It was as if their grief were for a loved one suddenly snatched from them, rather than for an ancient sorrow. The people fell to their knees and their tears scalded the cold marble floor.

But "head" Catholics deal in *symbols*, not in blood, sweat, and tears. We follow Christ, but painlessly and from a distance, making the Stations. We do not sweat to help build a church. We do not climb a mountain barefoot. We only read of these sacrifices — or write of them.

Yet I have always felt an intense sense of loss after witnessing one of these rituals, a numbing sense of loss that later forced me to look inward, somewhat sadly, to examine my own faith.

I do not believe that I am alone in my sense of loss. I believe that many "head" Catholics feel like prisoners of their own rationality and sense of decorum. They would welcome the tides of spiritual passion to free them from the narrow harbor of the mind.

"Unless ye become as little children...." Surely the words of Christ warned that sophistication may be a stumbling block; that we must be more in touch with our feelings. That faith is ultimately the *heart's* acceptance. For to be a pilgrim is to be as a child. To have a sense of awe and expectation. To believe the unbelievable. To climb the mountain. From a wheel chair. From a sickbed. A physical pilgrimage. A journey within. It doesn't matter. What matters is the feeling, the passion.

Next year in December there will be another pilgrimage to the top of the mountain in honor of Our Lady of Guadalupe. I would like to be there again with those

Indian and Mexican-American pilgrims. But more than that I would like to be *of* them. To share their expectations, their wonder, their joy. I would like to shed the shackles of the mind, becoming as a little child, allowing the imagination to soar to a rarer belief, a greater faith. I have been a "head" Catholic too long. It is time to make the Stations of the Heart.

4.

GHOST CHURCH

NOT FAR FROM GUADALUPITA in the northeastern part of New Mexico is an abandoned church. Adobe and squat, it has a reddish, corrugated roof with a bell tower rising like a hump from its back. Along one side, a fenced graveyard fans out twenty-five yards or so. Off to the west is the soft swell of a mountain. Green-clad and maternal, it watches over the deserted church in the valley — a church whose only living congregation consists of the birds that gather under its eaves.

The church is painted a shocking pink: it seems to blush at its own forsakenness. Yet it has a dreamlike, storybook quality: it seems set in memory, frozen in time, more like a work of the imagination than of human hands.

I first discovered the church in 1973. A wrong turn led me down a dead end, and I found myself drawn by the building's unusual color and the serenity of the place. As I stood looking at the ghost church, taking pictures and notes, I was startled to hear its bell toll three times. It was the Angelus, the call to prayer. The sound echoed through the valley to a scattering of birds and finally settled to silence. I checked my watch: noon. I decided to investigate. Descending a gentle hill, I entered the unlocked building.

Most of its furnishings — the Stations and statuary, the altar, and all but one of its pews — had been carefully removed. Stripped as it was, though, the church still had a holiness about it.

I almost stepped on several santos — wood carvings of Christ, the Holy Family, and the saints. Primitive, twisted, and angular, they were fashioned in the sharp geometries of pain and sorrow — crowns of thorns, crosses, and other images of violence and glory.

Suddenly I heard footsteps on the stairway leading to the bell tower. Spotlighted by a sunburst coming through a hole in the roof, I watched in astonishment as an old man with white hair came down the last few steps. When he reached the bottom he smiled. He did not seem surprised to see me.

He introduced himself. "I am Father Benitez," he said. "I am retired — if one ever retires from the service of God." His high, stiff collar gave him the appearance of a turtle peeking out from its shell.

I was still holding one of the wooden carvings I had picked up, the simple image of an agonized Christ. Quickly I set it down on a small table as the dust danced in a shaft of sunlight.

"Please," he said, "take it." He sat in the pew and motioned for me to sit beside him. "A souvenir," he told me. "I place them around for those who come." He took a deep breath. "This was my parish once," he said. "A parish of young and old. A parish of births, marriages, deaths. Of daily Masses. All Saints, All Souls. A parish alive with the grace of God." He shook his head. "But no more. Ten years ago the town died and the people left. And so I retired."

He smiled a thin, sad smile. "We wait together, Our Lady of Guadalupe and I. I am in good health for one so old, so the bishop lets me stay."

He went on to tell me how he prays for the deceased of the parish and tends the graves. And feeds the birds, "like St. Francis." And hand copies the church records, some going back almost a hundred years.

"But mostly I remember. I hold fast to things that should not be forgotten. Like a resurrection: I raise the past with my mind."

The priest told me about the miracle of the bell. It had been the climax to his ministry, perhaps to his life. One day in 1945 the bell had rung all by itself. No one knew how, or why. But people had hurried to church from all over the valley and Father Benitez had already begun a Mass of Thanksgiving when others heard the news over the radio: World War II had ended! Later, with a delegation of parishioners, he had gone to see the bishop about the miracle of the bell. But the evidence proved inconclusive. There were reports to be filed, people to be interviewed. There were debates and delays, and finally the matter was dropped, a victim of its own mystery.

"But the bell rang. All by itself," Father Benitez insisted. "I heard."

In the long silence that followed I seemed to hear a ringing echo.

"They rebuilt the steps," he said, almost apologetically. "They were afraid I might fall." He looked around and shook his head. "But the church is falling," he said. "Little by little — like the springtime snows with the sun shining. But as long as there are people who remember. . . ."

He smiled. "I painted it. But God gave us the valley, the mountains. And the bell. We mustn't forget the bell.

And those who sleep out back — myself too one day. Yes, it is a place to remember."

He smiled. "I watched you taking pictures, writing things down. *You* will remember. Perhaps one day you will return...."

His voice was insistent. As if people would remember this place by the sheer force of an old man's will. But it was hard to believe that even God would have business here — at a ghostly pink church where only the birds hymned. In a few short years there would be no one to remember. If Father Benitez was trying to lay that cross on my shoulders, I was an unlikely Simon. My roots were in another place.

Still, the old priest turned out to be right. Something did draw me back to those mountains, to that colorful church in the valley. Was it the memory of my first visit? Was it the miracle of the bell? Or the greater miracle of an old man's having elevated remembrance almost to a sacrament? I don't know. But four years later I returned.

I trembled as I approached a grave. It was scattered with wilted flowers. I knew who was buried there, for the dead have a language too. A man passionately devoted to memory had now become one. And now, as I stood over that mound of earth, I noticed for the first time the heavy silence of the place. The birds had left. And the bell was gone. The wind seemed no more than a hush in the pines. But Father Benitez was still a part of it all. He lived on as one of the prevailing spirits of the place.

I followed the row of crosses to the front door and went in. The interior was hollow as a cavern. But memory grew in the empty corners like cobwebs. And for a moment I saw him again — white hair, sad, heavy eyes.

I had returned. And over the years I have kept faith with the old priest and his church. For, you see, I have remembered. Perhaps I have even helped others to re-member: I wrote this story about him and you read it.

The pink church — do you see it too? The choir of birds? The bell ringing its call to prayer? Do you hear it shatter the silence?

You have, perhaps, become Father Benitez's latest convert. A convert to faith — and to memory.

TO AN INDIAN BORN IN 1890

Drowning-deep in yesterday,
He dreams of eagles caught in noon;
Of buffalo prairie thunder,
Of the Cherry Ripening Moon.
He dreams of *Paha Sapa*,[1]
And the bones in a Cottonwood tree
That never sing green with blooming.
He dreams of Wounded Knee.

He waits for the spotted eagle,
For the Christ on a buffalo white
Riding over the sage-strewn path
Like the moon in blackest night.
He waits for *WakaNtaNka*,[2]
For the Thunder Beings to call —
He waits like the prairie waiting
For anything at all.

---

[1] *Paha Sapa*: the sacred Black Hills of South Dakota.
[2] *WakaNtaNka*: the Great Spirit.

5.

THE VISION OF
NOAH JUMPING EAGLE

It was late in the summer of '64. The sky over the Dakota prairie was cloudless and a hurting blue.

Noah Jumping Eagle walked ahead of me leading the way toward the banks of the Little White River, which meanders darkly through the Rosebud Sioux Reservation, adding still another age-line to the face of the land.

Noah was a big man who had started to settle beneath the weight of his years. He had a classic Indian face with sharp, chiseled features and dark, shining eyes.

In most places I can think of, Noah would have been considered slightly mad or, at the very least, wildly eccentric. But here, in his mystical land among a mystical people, many considered him a holy man. He was as respected as a priest or surgeon might have been in another community. Mystics go with the territory.

Noah Jumping Eagle was a practicing Catholic, a pillar of his tiny parish in the Spring Creek community, but he was also an Indian and his imagination leaped to where the air was thinner and the more orthodox

feared to follow. He tracked his God like a hunter —
through the rim-rocked canyons, over eroded, tabletop
buttes, and even across the star trail.

He hungered after God — not just the *idea* of God, but
the living flesh. And finally in his sixty-seventh year, he
found God.

I believed him. I had known he was a man of faith
ever since the day we were discussing the drought in
the East, one of the worst in years. Water supplies were
dangerously low and the governor had declared a state
of emergency. When our conversation had trailed off
into a solemn shaking of heads, Noah startled me with
his simple proposal.

"Why don't you use prayer?"

"Some of us probably do pray," I answered vaguely.
"Farmers and people like that."

He shook his head. "I mean *together*," he said, as
though he were speaking to a child who didn't quite
understand. "A state day of prayer. When everybody
prays together. So God will be sure to hear."

Suddenly I thought I knew how Peter felt when the
cock crowed for the third time. How Thomas felt when
his finger found the nail holes. I, too, was one of little
faith.

As an outsider, an easterner, and an academic doing
research on the legends of the Sioux, I was a prisoner of
the culture that had shaped me. I saw through St. Paul's
glass darkly and might never come to see face to face.

It was a sad, even a frightening thought. Noah and
I shared the same God, yet he was free to run with the
hounds of heaven while I must wait, sifting the heart's
evidence against the head's.

"It is not far now," Noah said, breaking into my
thoughts, grinning his gold-toothed grin.

After another five minutes, Noah turned back to me.

"The holy tree," he said softly in Lakota, the language of the trans-Missouri Sioux.

I saw it. The holy tree. A huge cottonwood rising like a fountain. This was the tree, according to Noah Jumping Eagle, in which a vision of the Lord had appeared to him — not once, but every Friday throughout the summer.

Noah pointed to a V made by the meeting of the two largest branches on the tree. "There," he said pointing. "There is where He stands."

A shiver of expectation ran through me. At the same time, I remembered the words of a priest friend when I had told him about Noah's invitation to visit the holy tree.

"You won't see anything," he told me matter-of-factly. And then added, somewhat sadly I recalled, "Only those who have already found God can see Him like that." I didn't know what he meant then. I do now.

My friend had been a missionary to the Sioux for twelve years and had never ceased to wonder at their faith. It almost seemed as though he were jealous of their mystical ties with the land and the Great Spirit, who was also the Christ.

But the heightened sense of anticipation would not leave. And so we stood, looking up into the rustling cottonwood. I looked at my friend. In profile, with the sun pouring over his features, he looked like a hawk on fire. A predatory God-seeker.

Suddenly he slumped to his knees, bent his head, and struck his breast three times.

"My Lord and my God!" The words broke from him like a sob and I found myself kneeling beside him in the dust. As I knelt, I raised my eyes to the tree, searching the V of its branches. I saw nothing. Nothing but the upturning of silver leaves. In the back of my mind I kept hearing the echo of my priest friend's sad prediction: "Only those who have already found God can see Him like that."

Then, without any warning, Noah broke into song, "Great Spirit, have pity on me!"

He sang it four times and then four times four in a tuneless chant that was almost a wailing. His body shook. Then his voice faded and there were only the prairie sounds — the wind shaking the tree, the gurgling of the river, and the drone of locusts sawing on the afternoon.

After half an hour or so, Noah rose and without speaking a word, started back toward the tarpaper shack that he called home.

Later that night, in the flickering light of a kerosene lamp, Noah and I drank coffee. He was still visibly shaken from the effects of his visit to the holy tree. His gnarled fingers trembled around the warmth of the tin cup as a novice priest's might have trembled on the chalice. He had not spoken for hours, not since the song had burst from him. Now he was returning to the everyday world, a dream at a time.

"I didn't see anything," I said, my words falling awkwardly. I felt as though I were making my confession to an indifferent priest.

He continued to sip his coffee, holding the cup with both hands. He reminded me of a World War II photograph I had seen. A merchant seaman whose ship had been torpedoed from under him was on a rescue ship, clutching a mug of coffee. A blanket covered all but the dazed expression on his face.

"I saw nothing," I repeated.

Noah nodded, his face expressionless. Then the tight seam of his mouth moved like the opening and closing of a leather purse. "But He saw you."

That was all he ever said. When I left his cabin later that night, it was for the last time. The following summer when I returned, I learned that my friend had died during the winter. He had frozen to death. Somewhere by the holy tree.

I tried to find out where he was buried, but none of the Indians would talk about Noah. I checked the tribal offices and they had no details. Finally, I went to see my friend at the mission.

"Noah was a good Catholic," he told me. "He's in holy ground."

The next morning I went alone to the holy tree. It was a jewel of a day, very like the one on which Noah and I had made our visit together. As I came within sight of the river the feeling came over me that I had traveled in a giant circle and had returned to my point of departure. Memories drifted like lazy clouds across the span of time.

The tree seemed smaller somehow, as though I were seeing it through the wrong end of a telescope. I felt like a man returned to the scenes of his childhood who finds things dwarfed by absence.

I went to the far side of the tree. There was a mild depression in the earth there, a settling that I recognized. A chunk of rough jade as big as a man's fist and a withered branch from the holy tree were stuck in the ground. A prayer stick, its top painted red and dangling a turkey feather, leaned over at an odd angle.

I looked around, trying to imagine what the tranquil place was like with the winter wind lashing the kneeling tree. I tried to imagine what might happen to a man who fell through the ice and froze his legs. I tried; but the distance was too great. I was only a summer friend.

I felt that I should say something over the place. But

there was nothing to say. Noah had said it all when he knelt before the holy tree, borrowing the words of an anguished Thomas. I made the Sign of the Cross, the sign language for what I felt inside.

6.

A DEATH ON THE PRAIRIE

I BECAME A WITNESS TO THE OLD INDIAN'S DEATH quite
by accident. I was doing research for a book on the songs
of the Sioux and my work led me to his prairie shack on
the edge of the Badlands in South Dakota. One of my
informants in Pine Ridge Town had told me about old
Elijah, how he knew hundreds of songs, some going back
to pre-reservation times. That was all the encouragement
I needed, so I bought several bags of groceries and some
tobacco, and loading my tape recorder and camera into
my station wagon I set out, following the twin ruts that
led west across the stubbled prairie grass.

From the beginning it seemed like a journey back in
time. As I bounced along, leaving a wake of dust behind me, I watched the unfolding emptiness that swept
like a tide toward the horizon. A loneliness translated
into place. I passed an abandoned church brooding on a
hilltop, waiting for the slow stream of worshippers that
would never come again. A few miles later I saw an
isolated shack that had collapsed upon itself, its own
gray and formless monument to neglect. Overhead a
hawk floated across the setting sun in a bloody crucifix-

ion. And beyond, to the north and west, I could see the Badlands coming into focus, scarred and pitted like the surface of the moon.

Makoce Sica the Sioux called it, that stretch of gray desolation — the Badlands. And yet they found a beauty in that furious erosion: historically it had been a refuge and a retreat. A place to hide; a place to pray. A white person could only find it curious and frightening, a setting for science fiction. But to some Indians it was a sacred and holy place.

Elijah's home sat on the eastern edge of that ashen emptiness like a guardian, brooding over a geometry of lengthening shadows. His cabin of wood scraps and flattened tin cans seemed as temporary as the Gothic spires beyond seemed permanent. A reminder, perhaps, of the frailty of human efforts and the endurance of things created by the Great Spirit. Already his weather-beaten cabin listed from the constant wind. Already it had turned death gray and assumed the waiting attitude of prairie things that seemed to float on a sea of time.

Old Elijah was sitting on the careworn steps of his cabin, his creased, sagging face following the failing sun like a dark blossom. When I drove up in an explosion of dust he drew himself to his feet wearily, as though he had been interrupted from something important, and hobbled toward me in his worn cowboy boots.

I introduced myself to him, speaking in Lakota, which pleased him. I had heard he was a good singer, I told him, and knew many of the songs from the faraway times. He nodded and said it was good to hold on to the old things. Soon they would be as the wind in the buffalo grass. I unloaded the groceries, explaining they were a donation for any help he could give me with the songs, especially the old ones that were dying with the

people who were old. Soon they would be gone forever,
I said, like our yesterdays.

He nodded, a heavy sadness filling his eyes. "It is
good you have come today," he said softly. "For tomorrow I must go away."

I didn't pay much attention to his words at the time.
I supposed that his relatives or some friends were going
to pick him up and take him to Rapid City or maybe to
one of the Indian celebrations that filled the weekends
during the summer months. I never imagined he was
speaking of the big journey to the Spirit Land.

We sat outside on the steps watching the darkness fall.
In the west the outline of boiling clouds could be seen
and the distant lightning began stitching the earth and
sky. I knew the storm could hit or pass us by completely.
That is the way with prairie storms: they follow some
capricious compass of their own.

"*Wakinyan*," Elijah said, nodding toward the gathering storm. *Wakinyan*, the Thunderbird, whose eyes
flashed lightning and wings flapped thunder. It was a
good image, I thought, one that the poetic imagination
might easily accept in that mystical place.

In ten minutes or so the fury of the storm was upon
us. From inside the earth-floored cabin we could hear
the cascade of rain and the sharp explosions of thunder.
The wind ripped at the cabin like something gone mad
and drove the rain through the roof in silver splinters.
Elijah lit one of the kerosene lamps that hung from the
rafters, sat down in a huge chair that was shedding its
stuffing, and waited.

As I looked out the only window in the room into
the angry face of the storm, a quotation from the Bible,
from 2 Kings, crossed my mind: "...Elijah went up by
a whirlwind into heaven." It was strange, I thought,
how ancient words returned to light the moment, even

as the lightning turned the pages of night with a fiery finger. Elijah was the prophet who returned as the herald of the Messiah, the one referred to by Jesus in the Transfiguration. I looked at the old man across from me, wondering if he too could be a prophet of his people, the failing repository of their wisdom in legend and song.

I knew that the storm would force me to stay the night: the rains would turn even the ruts I had followed into a sea of mud. But in a way I was glad. I felt that there were things to be learned from this old man, who had lived through so much and who had stored so much of it in his heart.

After the storm passed and the air turned fresh and cool, we had a simple meal of canned tomatoes, bread, and coffee. Then we smoked in silence, a silence that was like a communion as he blew his smoke toward Earth, Sky, and the Four Directions to ensure the presence of the Great Spirit. Finally, he spoke in Lakota: "I can see that you have come with a good heart," he said in a frail and trembling voice. "I can see that you want to catch the songs of the people in that box so they will not be lost forever. So that the young people may remember. *Hecetu*. It is so. I will sing for you."

A few minutes later I turned on my battery-operated recorder and his high falsetto began to fill the room. Sometimes he accompanied himself on a small drum he held on his lap. His eyes closed, his head thrown back, he looked like one in a trance as the songs were drawn from memory like healing water from a deep well. Strong heart songs, ceremonial songs, healing songs, dream songs, council songs, honor songs, love songs — they all broke from his husky throat like something alive and imprisoned for a long time. Tears coursed down the furrows in his face as he sang the songs that had been handed down from his parents or grandparents, his loving legacy of dreams. He introduced each song in his own language and I did not interrupt him except to put a new tape into the recorder.

When the session was suddenly over, I had four hours of recordings and an old man's most precious possessions, the songs and prayers that had sustained him and his people. Then he told me about himself — how he had seen more than ninety winters, having been born in the same year that Crazy Horse was killed by the soldiers at Fort Robinson. How, for a brief moment in history, he had as a child known the old, free life. How he had lived through the massacre at Wounded Knee in December of 1890 and survived the terrible memory of his family killed, their bodies frozen in the grotesque sculptures of winter death. How he had seen his people delivered into bondage. How he had seen the old ways neglected, abandoned. How he had seen sacred things ignored and new ways and a new tongue take over. It was a liturgy of sorrow and pain that ended with the words: *Oyasin henala*, everything is gone. . . .

Not quite, I said to myself. Not quite everything is gone, Elijah. There is an old man's dignity and courage. There is an old man's caring. And sharing. There is an old man's faith. Such things do not die any more than the wind dies. . . .

I wish I had said these things to him. It is too late now.

Instead, I asked if I might stay overnight. He made a gesture with an arthritic claw of a hand: my house is your house. I went out, got my sleeping bag and returned. Old Elijah was pouring sand from tin cans onto the earthen floor of the cabin. I watched as he drew some things from a leather medicine bag — bird feathers, sage and sweetgrass, a buffalo skull, some colored bits of cloth, a bone whistle. He was making preparations

for a ceremony of some kind. I wondered why he didn't
go to bed and get some sleep. I looked at my watch. It
was after two in the morning and he was taking a trip in
a matter of hours perhaps. Suddenly he began to chant
softly in a heavy sing-song voice, something about the
hills and how they endure forever. Listening to the rise
and fall of his hypnotic rhythms, I fell asleep.

A slant of sunlight coming in the window awakened
me. I looked around for my host but he was gone. Perhaps he had left already on his trip, I thought. In the
center of the floor there was an altar of sand with the
Four Directions marked by tin cans containing minia-
ture flags of colored cloth. There were also feathered
prayer sticks stuck in small piles of sand. I had witnessed most of the ceremonies of the Sioux but I couldn't
identify the one Elijah had performed, perhaps was still
performing. Then I heard the sound of muffled drums
from somewhere outside, carried to me on the prairie
wind. I followed the sound and it led me behind the
cabin to a purification lodge made of willow branches
bent in the shape of an inverted bowl and covered with a
crazy patchwork of canvas and animal skins. The opening faced east and inside I could see clouds of steam
rising from the heated rocks.

Old Elijah was naked except for a breechclout. His
skin sagged on his bones and hung in folds like leather
clothing that was too large. The livid scars of count-
less flesh sacrifices to the sun and the spirits formed a
curious design on his chest, upper arms, and back. He
was seated like a frail Buddha, beating on his drum and
singing in a hoarse and croaking voice. This time I could
make out the words:

> This land is good.
> O Sun

> now
> for the last time
> come greet me again.

The old man was singing his death song!

Suddenly I could hear the echo of his words to me: "For tomorrow I must go away." I remembered, too, his solitary, early-morning ceremony with its song about the enduring hills. It had all been a ritualistic preparation for his death, and I was the inheritor of his last bequest — the blood truths of his songs. And now his death song was the last he would sing and it would go unrecorded except in my mind. I listened as he sang it again and again, over the beating of the drum and the wind song in the grass, his passionate song to the world that never sang to him, as pure and lyrical as any sounds of leaving.

The white man in me had questions: Why are you dying? How do you know? Is there anything that can be done? But the Indian in me said simply and softly: Leave him alone. It is a *wakan*, a sacred time, this leaving of one land for another. Everyone is alone at such a time. You will be, too.

But what about his family and friends? the white man insisted.

He has outlived them. They are of another time, another place. They have gone on ahead; they will be waiting on the star trail.

But how can I leave a dying man? There must be something that can be done.

There is. But only he can do it.

I stood there for a minute, watching, listening. Only once did Elijah look up from his song, and in that instant our eyes met and a truth passed between us, a truth so compelling that I turned immediately and walked back toward the cabin.

The next day, while having lunch at the Crazy Horse Cafe, I heard the first public reference to his passing. The place was crowded and people were talking about it.

"How'd he die?" someone asked.

"They don't know," a white man said. "They got to do an autopsy to find out the reason. Probably jus' old age, though. He must have been pushing a hundred."

"Autopsy won't show anything," an Indian said solemnly.

"Why not?"

"Not with Indians like Elijah. Old people like him die when it's time, that's all. There don't have to be reasons other than their own."

And that was the closest thing to a eulogy I was to hear.

I didn't attend Elijah's funeral or the interment. I had been a witness to the real ending that was also a beginning, and I felt that the public ceremony could add nothing to that singular experience. And it was painful for me to accept the idea that he might be buried in a crowded cemetery. Somehow I hoped he would find his rest on the hilltop at Wounded Knee or perhaps near his bleak and barren home, where the spirits of the place still whispered to the buffalo grass and the wind sang free. A truer requiem for a prairie prophet!

Some days later, there were a few columns about him in the weekly newspaper. A social worker had discovered the body when he had gone out to Elijah's isolated cabin to help him fill out some forms. Much was made of the fact that he was reputed to be the oldest Indian on the reservation at the time of his death and that he had been a survivor of Wounded Knee, the

very last. The article said there were no living relatives
and concluded with details of the funeral and burial.
The facts were all there, but somehow it wasn't the
truth. Any more than the autopsy report would be the
truth....

Old Elijah had sung me a better version!

7.

"WITHOUT MEMORIES WE ARE AS THE WIND"

IT HAPPENED ALMOST TWENTY YEARS AGO, on a hot July day, but I still remember it clearly. The old Indian woman was wearing canvas tennis shoes, an ankle-length dress, and a black shawl. She was carrying an open umbrella for protection against the fierce Dakota sun.

I stopped the car and asked her where she was going. To a small cemetery five miles west, she told me, on the edge of the Badlands. It was a long walk for a woman I guessed to be in her eighties, especially with the noonday sun beating down on the treeless prairie.

It turned out to be a half hour's drive. The gravel road stopped suddenly, continuing as two tracks across the open prairie. There were washouts, ruts, and bumps that slowed us to a crawl. But time is not so important on the plains. And the minutes were filled by an old woman's remembering.

She was going to visit her son's grave — to sing a song of remembrance and put a few sacred stones in the dust. He had been killed in the war, on some lonely Pacific island back in 1944, only eighteen when he died. She remembered the boy but had never known the man, and so her stories were seen through the eyes of her heart.

She told of his birth in the Moon of Falling Leaves, the white people's November. She told of the time he had wandered off at the Sun Dance at Pine Ridge and was lost for two hours; his first day at school after he had run from the school bus and hidden in the grass; his encounter with a rattlesnake near the wood pile; his First Communion.

I told her it was a long time to remember, to "throw the mind back," as the Sioux expressed it. I had lost friends in that war, had even seen them die, but now the sorrow had passed and there was only an absence, a kind of negative pain.

"We *must* throw the mind back," she insisted patiently. "Without memories we are as wind in the buffalo grass."

The cemetery was four dusty graves facing west. Two were unmarked, but my companion told me who was buried in them. One had died in World War I, a soldier. The other was a child who had died of the measles in the early '30s. Another gray, weathered stone carried the name of Elijah Jumping Elk and the dates 1900–1954. The fourth grave was her son's.

I stood awkwardly nearby as she reached in a pocket and withdrew two stones, kneeling to place them on the grave. I noticed there was a pile of them now, dropped over the years like solid tears. I knew that flowers would have wilted in an hour, and plastic substitutes weren't a part of her world.

Then she sang in Lakota a simple, trembling chant repeated over and over again:

> I remember Billy Two Hawk.
> He was a warrior
> With a strong heart.
> A son,
> I remember him.

That was all. That was all that needed to be said. The Great Spirit would know the rest. She made the Sign of the Cross and rose to her feet. I took her home.

By the time I returned to the reservation two years later she lay beside her son. I put a few stones on her graves — belated payment for some words she had given me one day, words that have become a part of my own silent requiems for nearly twenty years now.

On two occasions I have spoken her words aloud, once in anger and once in reverence.

The angry words were spoken to an overzealous salesman trying to sell me a word processor. I agreed with him that, in a certain sense, machines have a memory, that data can be stored and recalled later at the touch of a button. But in talking about what he called Random Access Memory, he concluded his pitch, "It has a memory like a mother's."

Instantly my own memory system was activated: an old Indian woman was dropping stones and prayers on a lonely grave near the Dakota Badlands. She was stooped and her leathery face was webbed with the lines of living. She didn't look much like the young woman operating the machine in the salesman's brochure. And the old woman's memory wasn't "Random Access." It was painfully selective.

A memory like a mother's?

"Not hardly," I told him.

"More like wind in the buffalo grass."

I never bought the word processor, perhaps because

memory is more sacred to me than it was twenty years ago. Perhaps because I feel memory should be accompanied by laughter or tears or some human feeling. It wasn't the salesman's fault. He was just doing his job. But in boasting of a machine's memory he had unknowingly tread on mine.

The other time I said her words aloud was at an All Souls' Day Mass.

During the homily my mind wandered. I was thinking of this holy day that the church has set aside for remembrance. And then in my mind the long parade of the dead began filing past, the faces that matched the list of names on the envelope I had put in the collection basket a week earlier. The parade started with a classmate in first grade and came up through the recent death of a good friend. Maybe fifty years of remembering.

And then it came to me that the church had elevated memory to a sacramental rite. The Mass itself was the celebration of a living memory. And there was the calendar: almost every day of the year was devoted to the memory of some saint. The collective memory of the Catholic church stretches back 2,000 years.

And it was then that I said it: "Without memories we are as wind in the buffalo grass." A few heads turned, but it was worth it to me — hearing her words spoken aloud again.

Growing older means living more intimately with memories. The eternal present may be good enough for youth but maturity demands more of us. Memories give a continuity, a sense of purpose to our lives. They echo back across the years those voices and images from the past telling us what we are and, if we are very lucky, what we should become.

8.

THE DAY THE SUN
STOOD STILL

H E WAS A YUWIPI MAN AMONG THE OGLALA SIOUX. A
shaman who invoked the spirits to heal, to find lost
things, and to predict the future. He was a devout Catholic too, seeing no contradiction at all in what some might
consider his double allegiance. At Mass he gave two of
the readings and when the celebration ended he went
outside to shake the hands of his brothers and sisters
and to wish them peace. And when there was a Yuwipi
meeting in the community he was there too with his
drum and rattle, sitting cross-legged in the pitch dark
crying in a shrill falsetto for the spirits to appear — the
spirit of *cetaN*, the hawk, *mato*, the bear, and *waNbli*, the
eagle.

"Who controls the spirits?" I remember asking him
once.

"*WakaNtaNka*, the Great Spirit," he answered. And
then he added with a half-smile: "You know — Jesus."

At the time I was a collector of songs and I was especially interested in his Yuwipi songs, his songs of healing

and his songs calling the spirits. I was also interested in a Winter Count made of deerhide that he had hanging on the wall of his prairie shack. The deerhide was filled with pictographs, primitive, one-dimensional drawings, each one representing an event for which a particular year would be remembered — a kind of picture calendar and diary all in one. He had started it in 1933 when he was ten years old, and the picture for that first year showed crops withering under a black cloud. I remembered what was called the "dust bowl" myself: it had drifted east to show itself as a sickly yellowish haze before the sun. And I still remembered John Steinbeck's fictional account in *The Grapes of Wrath*.

Then my eye shifted to the last of the drawings, a drawing that showed the fierce, burning eye of the sun at its zenith and directly beneath it the stick figures of a man and a woman with white hair.

"What does that one mean?" I asked him.

"That was last year," he answered. "The day the sun stood still."

His words struck a distant chord in my memory. The Old Testament, the Book of Joshua. The young warrior had prayed to the Lord to have the sun stand still in the heavens, giving the people of Israel more daylight, more time to avenge themselves on the enemy.

"Joshua — he made the sun stand still — or rather he asked the Lord to do it," I said aloud, remembering.

My friend nodded. "He wanted the day to last so he could defeat the enemy." He pointed to his own drawing. "But in this one the sun stood still for peace, for mercy and for love."

I asked him what he meant and he told me this story, a story I re-tell as I remember it today, many years later. A story I try to tell in his own words:

An old woman lay dying in her home near Wounded

Knee. She had some sickness in her body, but most of it was in her heart because her son was a soldier in Vietnam. He was her only son and she was always worried about him and praying for his safe and speedy return. She didn't want him to go to war but he had reminded her what she could not forget — that all his ancestors were great warriors and he could not let them down. They might be looking down from the other side, watching for him to be brave against the enemy. His father had died a hero in World War II and the American Legion Post on the reservation had been named after him. And hadn't he passed it daily? And sometimes gone in to look at the display case in the lobby where his father's Congressional Medal of Honor lay on black velvet? Hadn't he made his daily pilgrimages to the place where his father's memory was kept under glass. His father had left burning memories and high standards to live by — and to die by, if necessary.

When the young man got to Vietnam he did some brave things for which he was given medals. There were stories about him in the Rapid City newspaper and even as far away as Omaha. And sometimes his picture was on the television news, the picture he had taken for his mother — in his uniform, looking proud and handsome like a young warrior from the faraway times. On the reservation he helped old men remember and young men have pride.

But his mother grew weaker and weaker.

There is a sickness that comes from the inside, the heart. There is a sorrowing that no medicine will cure. There is a loneliness that is as fatal as any plague. The WasicuN ("whites") do not always believe it — looking as they do for reasons that they can examine. But the Indians know that the heart is a delicate thing, delicate as the wings of the butterfly.

When it was certain that the soldier's mother was dying the young man was sent for and put on an airplane for home. But it would take many hours for him to cross the great water and the old woman was growing weaker by the hour.

It was then that some among the Indian people came to me and asked to give them the greatest gift — the gift of time. They wanted me to make time stand still so that the soldier would come home before the old and sick mother died.

I thought about it and I prayed over it but no answers came to me. In all my years in calling the spirits no one ever asked me to do that. I had healed through the spirits. I had found a body that had been drowned in the river. I had predicted that the rains would come in late summer. But I had never stopped time in its flight. And then it was that I remembered the part in the Bible, the Old Testament, about Joshua. And the words came through like printed words in my mind: "And there was no day like that before or after it, that the Lord hearkened unto the voice of a man — "

And so I prayed to the Lord Jesus and asked him for this thing — that the soldier get here in time to see his mother, and I made up a song that I sang and it went like this: "Sun, stand still in the sky." And I sang it over and over again. And as I was singing the dark clouds rolled in and I could not see where the sun stood in the sky, but it seemed that, in my heart, there was a slowing and then a stopping. I felt like I had died and then come back to life and I could not account for what happened in between the time of leaving and the time of returning.

The Lord answered my prayers. I do not know if he used the spirits or not. But the soldier landed in California and then took a plane to South Dakota and then a helicopter to the reservation hospital. There was time, don't you see? He and his mother were together for an hour before she died and that is time enough to come together again and say what is in the heart. And so I thanked the Lord for what he had done and I thanked Joshua for giving me the idea of asking the Lord for the sun to stand still. Not for killing but for saving. Not for death but for tender mercies and love.

And that was how it was that I called that year by the name the Day the Sun Stood Still.

An hour after my friend had finished his story we were on our way to Mass, walking the dusty path to the small, wooden church in a remote corner of the reservation. We were talking about other things but my mind was still on his story, a story of almost perfect faith in a sometimes faithless world. And before his faith I suddenly felt a great humility and even an envy, wishing that I could somehow suspend my own rationality, if only for the length of time it took him to tell his story.

We had come up over a dusty knoll and the prairie seemed to spread out before us as far as the eye could see. The sky was a bright blue. My friend tugged at my sleeve and nodded toward the eastern sky where I saw what could only be an eagle soaring on unmoving wings like something frozen in flight.

"*WaNbli,*" he said, smiling faintly, pronouncing the word slowly and with reverence, as though something had been settled in his mind. As if, for him, there was some necessary and logical connection between the appearance of the lordly bird in the sky and his story about the sun standing still. As if the eagle in the sky was a punctuation to mark an end to his story.

I followed his gaze and echoed: "*WaNbli.*"

But somehow it was a hollow amen that echoed in my heart.

9.

A CONFLICT OF INTERESTS

HE WAS FOUND UNCONSCIOUS ON A BACK ALLEY street in the ghetto of a large eastern city and then brought by ambulance to the emergency room of one of the city's hospitals. He had either been savagely beaten or he had fallen from an abandoned shell of a tenement building that towered overhead. The doctors pronounced him a dying man.

They went through his pockets for identification but found only a few things, a few curious enough to interest the police. His clothes were the clothes of a poor man — blue denim work shirt and faded, torn jeans. But there were a few clues: he was wearing high-heeled Western boots and not more than ten feet from the body was a black Western hat with a hawk's feather in the band. There was another clue — the man looked like a Native American. There were the classical features: high cheekbones, a sharp Roman nose, dark skin and long, black hair.

He was wearing a plain, silver cross around his neck. But what the police found interesting and suspicious was what he had in his pockets. In addition to one dollar and seventeen cents in change he had a shriveled spider in a plastic pill bottle and three peyote buttons — a hallucinatory agent that was considered a "controlled substance." They put their clues together and speculated that the victim was an Indian, probably from the West or Southwest and that he might be involved in drugs and perhaps in some mysterious cult of native origins. Later, while he was in the Intensive Care Unit, hooked up to machines that seemed to be sucking the life from him rather than keeping him alive, a nurse who had once lived in the state of South Dakota heard him murmuring in his restless inner wanderings and thought that the language he spoke might be Lakota, the language of the Teton Sioux. And it was because of her observations that I became involved.

Since the early 1960s I had been involved with the Lakota — as a student, writer, and friend. I had written three books about the people and their culture and knew the language fairly well. Both the hospital people and the police thought that if the victim regained consciousness, someone could talk to him and find out who he was so that the family could be notified and the other leads pursued by the police. They got in touch with me through the academic community, asking for my help. I agreed because I knew how important the family was in the life of a Lakota, especially when he was a stranger in a strange land, alone and dying. Also I remembered something an old friend had told me back during my first summer on the reservation. He told me that even though an Indian might die away from home he was always buried back home on the reservation. His final resting place was where his roots were and so he became a part of the web of life that was so sacred to him.

When they told me about the peyote buttons and the spider in a plastic bottle, the picture became clearer. The

Indian might well have been a member of the Native American Church, in which peyote plays an important part in the ritual.

"What about the cross around his neck?" someone asked me. "Doesn't that contradict what you're saying?"

I explained that the Native American Church was Christian as well as native. It was a paradox to the *WasicuN*, white people, but not to the Indians. It was the same with the spider, *Iktomi*, the Trickster of their legends: *Iktomi* was probably his totem, his talisman, the source of his power. That was why he carried it around with him in a plastic bottle. In the old days he would have had a "medicine bundle," a decorated leather pouch to carry his totems in, especially when he went into battle.

I told the police that the peyote buttons had nothing to do with dealing drugs — although I am not sure that they believed me. And I told them that the spider in a bottle was not important except to him, a kind of good luck charm and more. I knew that my explanations were simplistic and I knew that what I hadn't said had more to do with the truth of the matters. But I knew I couldn't get them to understand: they were cultures apart.

Even before he regained consciousness I visited his bedside. His head was a turban of bandages and there were some heavy, purple marks and bruises on his face. An I.V. tube was in one arm and some clear liquid dripped from a bottle suspended over him — a drop at a time like some Chinese water torture. A red light from the machine made waves and a red dot pulsed at regular intervals. And there was a constant noise that came from the machine, a humming noise that was both reassuring and frightening — frightening because like a heartbeat it could stop at any time. And then there would only be a huge, electronic hush and a line that did not wave. And along with all the lights and sounds from the machine there was one small and fugitive thing from outside that had snuck in through the window shade — a broken ray of sunshine that entered and was projected against the pale turquoise wall.

In his delirium he mumbled words about home, family, and *WakaNtaNka*, the Great Spirit, but there were no logical connections. Nothing that made sense to me. He spoke of Eagle Butte, Wounded Knee, the hawk, and *Iktomi*, the Spider. He spoke of his mother, father, and especially about *UNci*, his grandmother. He spoke words and phrases, but not sentences, not ideas. I sat and waited. From time to time I would lean close to him and say something in Lakota, hoping to bring him back from where he wandered. But he did not respond.

On the third day, and while I was there, he opened his eyes and looked around him like a startled Lazarus waking up in a place he did not know. His eyes blinked at the red eye in the machine that was blinking back at him. He watched the liquid as it dripped, dripped, dripped — either giving him something or taking it away.

As I leaned closer his eyes found mine and lit on them like a dark butterfly on a flower. At first they seemed to ask questions that could not be put in words, questions about the prairie, the wind, sun, and sky. Then slowly, deliberately his lips began to move silently and after a minute or two a sound broke from them, a song sung in a rusty, hoarse, and faraway voice, a voice drawn from some inner spring far beneath the surface of his being. I put my ear down closer to hear his words. And finally, after nearly an hour I leaned back, content that I had done my best in putting his words into English. Everything but the *why* and the wonder of it all!

He was singing his Death Song and it went like this:

"Come to me, O Sun, for the last time. Come to me, O Wind, and I will follow!"

It was a song he had composed for his leaving of this world for another. And I wondered once again as I had wondered over the years at an art form that was forged in the white heat of one's dying. That was at once a part of life, a part of death. Certainly it must be the purest and most intense poetry in this world! He sang it over and over again and I knew he probably would not stop singing until death finally silenced him. Suddenly I heard a noise from behind me. I turned and saw a young doctor in a T-shirt and running shoes standing in the doorway. He wore a stethoscope around his neck that looked like a dead snake, and he carried a clip board that he seemed to be studying.

"What's he saying?" the doctor asked. "Can you understand?"

"It's a song," I explained. "A Death Song."

The young man's face was a question mark. "A song?"

I nodded. "A very special song," I said. "His last."

"Ask him who he is and where he's from," the doctor ordered, somewhat impatiently I thought. "We want to notify his family." And then he added urgently: "He hasn't got long."

"He knows that," I said. "That's why he's singing."

"Ask him what I said. The police want to know."

I looked back to the Indian. His face was a mask of peace. His thoughts and feelings seemed light years away. I noticed that his eyes were open and focused on the spot of sunshine on the wall as though it had been the burning eye of the Great Spirit. The song was still coming from his lips, and he seemed to be tasting the words as they came, tasting all the prairie things he had not known — in how many winters? I could not tell.

Savoring again the sun, the wind, the smell of sage and sweetgrass, the gathering of eagles in the clear sky.

I knew that the time for him was *WakaN* — holy, sacred, and mysterious. A time of leaving. Perhaps even a time of arriving. The most important time of his life. And his eyes shone as if all the energy of his spirit were suddenly focused like a burning glass on those moments of departure. He sang in a husky, droning falsetto that seemed to have no end. And, listening, I was suddenly taken back across the miles, across the years to a prairie kind of living and a prairie kind of dying too. And I saw again Martha Lone Eagle in the alien sterility of a hospital room and heard again her song of leaving. And I heard an old man singing his greeting to the Morning Star. And I heard the birth cries of tiny Jimmy Crow Eagle as he came into the world. I heard the prairie wind as it sang through the wires. And I heard too a Christian hymn as it came from a plain wooden church on the prairie....

"Ask him!" the doctor ordered again as he crossed the room and checked the blinking lights, the waving lines. "His name and where he's from. Who we should notify."

I looked back at the eyes of the dying man, and he talked to me through them. He had understood the doctor's words — but they were not important to him for reasons of his own. The words of his song were important. His departure. The waiting spirit trail. The spot of sun on the wall. The rest was the world's business.

"One world at a time," his eyes seemed to plead. "I must be about the business of moving on."

I didn't know what to do. The physical world was pulling me one way and the spirit world another. The Indian was pulling me one way and the white man another. The past and the present. Jesus and *WakaNtaNka*. *Iktomi*, the spider, and the hawk. A humming, blinking machine and a spot of sun on the wall. There was a warring in me that I did not understand.

"Ask him!" the doctor ordered once again.

But when I bent closer this time I noticed his song had stopped with a kind of gurgle. His eyes were still focused on the sliver of sun — a burning, passionate focus as though on eternity itself. Uncertain and confused I looked over at the machine as though for confirmation of something I didn't quite understand. But the waves had stopped and so had the humming sound. It was as though I was standing by the ocean and the tides had suddenly stopped. Only the red eye continued to blink, as though taking a long, last look at what had been.

10.

THE YUWIPI CULT

A *YUWIPI* (U-WEE-PEE) MEETING is a kind of native divine madness complete with darkened rooms, spirits, flesh offerings, wild singing and drumming, healing, prophecy, magic, and, usually, a dog feast. The cult flourishes today on the Rosebud and Pine Ridge Sioux Reservation in South Dakota. It also invades the precincts of fashionable, middle-class homes in areas adjacent to the reservation. And there have been regular meetings held in such faraway places as Denver, Los Angeles, and New York City.

The New York Times once carried a feature story entitled "In the Land of the Rosebuds, *Yuwipi* Still Counts." The article tells how the two candidates for the office of tribal chairman each consulted his one or more *Yuwipi Wicasa* (*Yuwipi* Men) and attended *Yuwipi* meetings in order to influence the outcome of the tribal elections through the intervention of the spirits. Both candidates were mixed bloods in their forties, highly intelligent, sophisticated, widely-traveled, and both had held offices of responsibility before, on a national as well as a tribal level. One of the candidates has since written an articulate, well-received book on the fifteen-year history of the Rosebud Reservation's struggle for self-determination.

Why then should each of these men sit in the pitch-black room of some isolated shack tucked away in the brown folds of the prairie — a room exploding in drumbeats and the high, nasal cries of the Indian singers? Why should they sit there on a rolled-up rug like Buddhist suppliants awaiting the entrance of the *Yuwipi*, the spirit beings?

The answer lies in the vitality and psychological appeal of *Yuwipi*: in what it *means* and what it *does*.

Yuwipi, in the Lakota language, means "they wrap him up" and refers to the practice of wrapping and tying the shaman so that he may be set free by the spirits. The name is also used to refer to the spirits themselves. The origins of the cult appear to be lost in the dim past but it has probably evolved from the "dream cults" of the Indians of the Plains, cults that feature shamans who perform magic and healing through control of personal spirits. Parallels between *Yuwipi* ritual and those of the Ojibway and Cree Shaking Tent cults have been observed. *Yuwipi*, then, has probably developed from a diffusion of ceremonies like these.

The purposes of the *Yuwipi* meeting are to cure illness, to find lost articles, to prophesy, and, quite unofficially, to put on an exciting, séance-like show designed to relieve the boredom of reservation life.

The person who wants the help of the spirits approaches the shaman, frequently in the traditional way: by offering him a pipe or a pouch of tobacco. While the *Yuwipi Wicasa* smokes, the suppliant relates his case and the reasons for his request. It may be that he has lost his wallet with a week's pay in it. It may be that he hasn't heard from his son who is far away and wants to know if he is safe and well. Or it may be that his hand is taking the shape of a claw from the twisting pain of arthritis and he wants to be cured. "There are as many reasons as there are people," one old *Yuwipi* Man told me.

If the *Yuwipi Wicasa* decides to take the case he gives the suppliant a list of articles to buy for the meeting. The list usually includes a specified number of yards of colored cloth, pouches of tobacco, and food for a feast — canned tomatoes, bread, potatoes, pastry, and perhaps a few watermelons, if they are in season. The *Yuwipi Wicasa* will furnish the meat: a young dog strangled and boiled in water.

The person who requests the meeting may expect to spend from fifteen to twenty dollars on these supplies, depending on the number of people attending the meeting. That person may also expect raised eyebrows from the clerks in the trading post where the supplies are bought. Although the *Yuwipi* cult affects an exaggerated secrecy, most people on the reservation know what the purchases are for.

The time and place of the meeting are spread by way of the "moccasin grapevine." The time is usually when it grows dark. The place may be an isolated cabin, ten miles and five cattle fences from town. The windows of the cabin have been covered with bits of old rug or burlap bags. When the people begin to arrive there is only a single kerosene lamp hanging from a nail on the exposed rafters, a lamp constantly under attack by a flurry of summer insects.

All Christian statuary has been removed from the room: on the place where a crucifix hung there is the pale ghost of a cross. The furniture has been taken from the room too. The rugs have been rolled up and set against the longest walls. In the center of the room is a raised earthen altar. At each of the cardinal points a large, dirt-filled tin can holds a pennant of colored cloth tied to a stick. Two other pennants — green for earth and blue for sky — are placed in larger cans where there are also sticks to which eagle feathers are attached. Other ceremonial objects include a folded quilt, a rope of sweetgrass, assorted herbs, a single-edged razor blade, and a bucket of water in which floats a metal dipper.

When the guest and participants are seated cross-legged on the floor, their backs resting against the rolled-up carpets, the *Yuwipi Wicasa* and his assistant enter. The shaman proceeds to arrange a twenty-foot string of tied tobacco packets called *caNli wapahta* around the perimeter of the earthen altar. These represent tobacco offerings to the spirits; the women have spent most of the day pinching the tobacco into tiny wads of paper and tying them so they resemble rosary beads. The rest of their time has been spent in preparing the feast to follow the meeting.

While the kerosene lamp flickers and throws sharp geometries on the walls and the faces of the people assembled, the *Yuwipi Wicasa* relates the story of how his power came to him. He tells this in Lakota and later, in deference to the few whites in attendance, translates what he has said into *WasicuN*, English. His power comes from *WaNbli Gleska*, the Spotted Eagle, seen in a vision when he was a young man. A single eagle's feather is tied in his shoulder-length hair, token of the mystical covenant between man and bird.

The shaman's assistant passes out sprigs of sage, first to the men sitting on one side of the room and then to the women sitting opposite them. Infants and young children cling to the mothers, their dark eyes wide, shining with anticipation.

The *Yuwipi Wicasa* lights the rope of sweetgrass and waves it around to purify the people and the sacred cer-

emonial objects. He does this with all the solemnity of a
priest consecrating a new church building. Then he fills
the pipe and presents it to the Earth, Sky, and the Four
Directions, thus insuring the presence of *WakaNtaNka*,
the Great Spirit.

A man and two middle-aged women step forward to
hold the pipe close to them while the shaman picks up
the razor blaze. Then he proceeds to cut small pieces
of flesh from their upper arms and shoulders, depositing
them in three gourd rattles as offerings to the spirits. The
votaries flinch and look away as the blade slices Vs from
their flesh. The assistant stands by like a nurse, wiping
away the blood with bundles of wadded sage.

Each of the votaries then explains the reasons for the
flesh sacrifice. The man's brother has been injured on
the job. He gives twenty pieces of flesh to the spirits
for his recovery. The two women are sisters and their
mother is soon to have a serious operation. They have
given their flesh for her.

The shaman's assistant again passes out sprigs of silvery, perfumed sage so that the *Yuwipi* will recognize
the faithful. He instructs the people to place a stem behind the left ear. Then he crosses to the kerosene lamp
and snuffs it out, plunging the place into a cavernous
darkness.

The opening chant begins. The nasal voices, pitched
high, approach a plaintive whine. The small, one-sided
drums begin to explode alternately. The women wait
for the chorus and then join in, their voices pitched an
octave above the men's:

> *Oyate kiN hoye heyaya mani pe;*
> *Oyate kiN hoye heyaya mani pe...*
> The tribe sends a voice as they walk;
> The tribe sends a voice as they walk...

The opening song has ten verses, building to a wild, hypnotic crescendo. A frightened child begins to scream — a shrill, piercing cry that is finally drowned in the high keening sounds of the women. Then, after more than ten minutes of singing, the drums stall to silence — a heavy, ear-ringing silence like the stillness of an afterstorm. The lamp is lit but there is no spiritual light: the *Yuwipi* have failed to appear. There is a moaning and cries of disappointment by the believers as they wait expectantly for what will happen next.

The *Yuwipi Wicasa* tries again. This time he will be wrapped in a quilt and bound hand and foot with leather thongs. He tells the people that the *Yuwipi* will come and release him. The shaman's assistant and several men volunteers wrap and tie him securely. As the darkness drops again the muffled voice of the shaman is heard invoking the spirits, calling them by name: *"Iktomi!"* (Spider!); *"CetaN INyaNke!"* (Running Hawk!); *"WaNbli Gleska!"* (Spotted Eagle!) . . .

His voice sounds far away, crying out from the dark — a forlorn, disembodied cry from a deep well. He begs the *Yuwipi* to come to the aid of the people through him. The women join him in a chorus of moans, a chorus that swells like wind over prairie grass.

Suddenly, there are whirring sounds — as through the room were full of angry dragonflies. Small greenish spurts of light burst before the eyes. Heads duck, screaming to avoid them. Under the heavy pulse of the drums, the shaman cries out like a soul in torment: *"TuNkashila! TuNkashila!"* Grandfather! Grandfather! He invokes *WakaNtaNka*, whom he calls Grandfather, the rough equivalent of the Christian God-the-Father. The hearts of the votaries quicken to the driving, pulsating drumbeats, racing toward some mystical climax. Then, when it seems as though the sound barrier has been shattered, the drums pause, sound twice more and then stop as an inverted bell of silence settles on the place.

The voice of the *Yuwipi Wicasa* comes from the darkness, now loud and clear with promise. He reveals what the *Yuwipi* have told him. The man's brother, injured on the job, will recover. The *Yuwipi* have told him that he will be home from the hospital in a few months. The mother of the sisters will be made well by her operation. She will live more than eighty winters, the spirits promise.

Suddenly, there is light! Cries of surprise and delight greet the *Yuwipi Wicasa* as he reveals himself free of his bonds, standing before them. Hearts leap! The *Yuwipi* have kept their promise!

The *Yuwipi Wicasa* sings a "doctoring" song over those who wish to be cured — an arthritic old man and a child with an eye disease. Then the medicine pipe is passed around. Everyone — man, woman, and child — takes a puff and utters the ceremonial phrase: *"Mitakuye oyasin!"* My relatives all! The water is passed around in the same clockwise direction as the pipe. Everyone drinks from the same dipper, repeating *"Mitakuye oyasin!"* With the communion of the smoke and the water, the ceremony ends. The hunger of the spirit has been fed. Now comes the *SuNka*, or Dog Feast. The people eat, relax, and socialize until early in the morning.

Walking out into a grinning, gold-toothed night of stars, a night alive with the restless murmur of the constant wind, things become clearer. It has been a wild night, filled with magic and hope. The placid, steepled churches caught in the ashen burning of the moon seem to raise an admonishing finger skyward, never having known such abandon. There, the hymns have swelled and fallen again like soft rain heard from a distance. The deep-throated organ has soothed. Words have fallen on the heads of sinners, healing old wounds. A whispered chorus of prayers has risen gentle like a promise. A steeple of sound. The children have cried, but in a special glass enclosure called a "crying room..."

But the real hunger is for the *drums* — the heart's quick tune — that stirs the blood-tide to swell the banks of time and loss. The real hunger is for *song* — song that rises on a scream to pierce the vast, sullen indifference of the Dakota sky. The real hunger is for the *spirits* — spirits that flash green and angry, frightening the people into hope.

The real hunger is for *magic* — magic to raise the people to a more vital level of awareness. To lift them from the rutted flats of tedium and apathy to where the air is thin and the spirit soars free as an eagle, cut loose from the bonds of necessity. A moment's resurrection.

Yuwipi feeds the hunger of the Indian spirit. No matter that most of its devotees are Christians. They will be at Mass or Worship on Sunday. They will follow the slow tolling of the bells through dusty streets. They will bow their heads and whisper their written prayers. Sing their softer hymns shyly. Listen to old stories of a distant Galilee....

But tonight? Tonight their ears are bent to a different ground. Tonight the drums throb of more ancient things. Of blood instincts and timeless places. Of bloody hawks on the fire-altar of Noon. Of buffalo gods, drumming thunder on the plains. Of eagles and Thunder Beings riding the lightning of the sky.

Tomorrow they will return to tread their weary circles in the dust.

Tonight let the echoes cry!

11.

MASS HERE, MASS THERE

BEFORE I WENT TO THE ROSEBUD SIOUX RESERVATION in south-central South Dakota, my Catholicism had been middle class. That is, rational, affluent, organized, and convenient.

My home parish of St. Thomas was located in the fashionable suburbs. Its congregation was highly educated and so was its clergy. Its buildings, a new church, a rectory, and an elementary school, rose like golden islands in a sea of well-manicured grass. The church was cool in the summer and warm in the winter.

Most of the Gothic interior was done in shining white marble. There was an elaborate sound system that caught even a whisper in its bellows and shivered it around the church until it finally died on an electronic hush. There was an organ that trembled the silence and bells that chimed gentler tunes. The pews were comfortable and the kneeling benches were padded. Even the stained-glass saints that paraded the walls seemed to wear a richer sun in their robes of glory.

I do not mean to imply that there was anything unchristian about such dignified opulence. None of its splendor was rendered to Caesar. All of it was rendered to God. But it was a dramatic contrast to what I experienced while worshipping among the Sioux.

In the summer, the church bells of the tiny reservation community shattered the silence. Before 10 a.m., when the bells first sound for the 10:30 Mass, the June day seems suspended on a breath. The dusty, unpaved streets are like the furrows of a deserted farm. Even the constant prairie wind seems but a whisper, nudging a stick-ball of tumbleweed down the empty street.

The bells are nagging. There is no escape from their solemn summons.

A half mile from the church, the door of a wooden shack opens slowly and a black-shawled old woman steps on skinny legs into the dust. Beaded sneakers stick out from under the hem of her ankle-length dress. In one hand she carries a black umbrella to be used against the noon sun on her return. In the other hand she carries a worn prayer book written in the Lakota language and a knobby, black wooden string of beads dangling a crucifix. The old woman's face is the color of polished dark wood.

As she shuffles painfully down the street toward the ringing of the bells, her shoes kick up tiny explosions of dust behind her. She feels the sun on her face but she does not raise her eyes. The cataracts growing there have cruelly limited her vision to the length of her own shadow in the dust.

A man catches up to her. He wears a blue denim work shirt, blue denim jeans, and a black Western hat sprouting an eagle's feather. His dark eyes look out sadly from beneath its wide brim.

The man too is old, older than the woman who is his

wife. He has the same dark skin, the same well-deep eyes, the same timeless dignity — almost the dignity of a mountain sculptured by the centuries.

Others have started to appear in the street. A middle-aged couple, each holding the hand of a young child, follow the bells. The children dance beside them, their dark button eyes shining with a Sunday excitement.

Old Frank Horn Bear hobbles down the street, already having walked the four long miles from his isolated prairie shack near Grass Mountain. Last night he was a native priest invoking the spirits of the bear, the hawk, and the deer in his attempts to prophesy and cure. But today he has left the darker world of the spirits and leans on a heavy stick to help him find God. His simple faith is beyond paradox.

In front of the church there is a scattering of battered, dusty cars and pickup trucks. Most of them are ten to twelve years old and rattle along in various stages of disrepair. Wooden racks on the roofs hold the few bald spare tires that make the difference between riding and walking. A few of the cars are new and shiny, bearing the colors of faraway places on their license plates. New York. Vermont. California.

The church is an old, plain wooden building, wearing a new coat of white paint. Its architecture is Prairie Gothic. It has the stark innocence of a little girl in her First Communion dress.

The people, twenty or so, climb the worn, creaking steps. Inside, the church is equally plain. The Stations tell their story around the bare walls. The pews, stiff and formal, wait before a flickering of candles. By the side of the altar, St. Joseph holds a T-square in one hand and balances the Christ Child in the other. There is the ghost of a smile on his face. He seems to approve of the crude carpentry of the dedicated Indians who built the church. "It is finer than halls of marble," his smile assures them, "because you built it with your own hands."

The altar is covered with buffalo hides sewn together. The words *WakaN, WakaN, WakaN* (Holy, Holy, Holy) are printed in brilliant yellow across the front. The candles are set in buffalo horns.

Behind the altar hangs a huge crucifix. The Christ crucified is an Indian Christ. His long hair is braided; the eyes are dark almonds; the cheekbones are high and shine a gun-metal blue.

Beneath the crucifix is a peace pipe suspended from leather thongs. On one side wall is a painting of a huge Thunderbird and, on the opposite wall, a conical tipi covered with a sharp geometry of designs.

The Indian lay reader enters and the congregation rises to a chorus of squeaks from the wooden benches. Then the priest appears, flanked by two Indian altar boys. The priest wears beaded vestments, a gift from the people of the community. He wears them proudly, knowing that stiff fingers worked many long winter nights sorting the tiny beads.

The chorus begins the first hymn, "Nearer, my God to Thee," sung in the Lakota language.

Looking around at the people, one is impressed with their poverty, their faith, and their dignity. The people who are assembled here are the poorest of the poor. Most of them have missed meals or filled empty stomachs with heavy starches — Indian fry bread washed down with coffee. The hands of both men and women are rough and calloused; the fingers are thick and stiff. The faces are the faces of a people who have suffered and who wear the marks of their suffering proudly, as a soldier wears his medals. A dark flame still burns like a jet in their eyes no matter how creased and leathery the skin. In those eyes there is the smoldering triumph of having endured.

The children are as restless as all children, anxious to be off and running knee-deep in June. Their dark eyes flash impatience.

The homily is short, but not sweet. It deals in hard, realistic prose with the evils of alcohol, perhaps the severest social problem on the reservation. The priest talks of broken dreams and broken lives. He cites a member of his congregation who has mended his life by swearing off. He talks of others who drank themselves into early graves. He talks of families abandoned. Of cattle dead of thirst because no one checked the windmills that pumped them water. Of crops unharvested. Of men in jail for crimes committed while in a drunken stupor. Of twisted bodies pulled from the wreckage of automobiles.

His staccato address is punctuated with the guttural, assenting *haus* (yes) and *hecetus* (it is so) of the males in the congregation. The priest concludes his brief sermon in a passionate burst of Lakota: *"YatkaN sni yo!"* Drink not!

The few tourists present are surprised. There has been no mention of God in the homily. No attempt to relate the Sunday Gospel to the lives of the people. No instruction in matters liturgical. Just an old priest's tirade against liquor.

But the words were not addressed to tourists. The Indians approve. There is not one among them whose life has not been touched by the curse of drink.

When the collection is taken, the men squirm to get their hands into the tight pockets of their jeans and the women open their small, worn purses to select one of their precious coins. The ringing of silver on wicker is the only sound for a few minutes as the basket is passed from hand to hand. One of the tourists puts a bill in the basket. No one turns to look. It would be poor manners to notice and the Indians would not want to embarrass their guests.

Later in the Mass the priest says: "Let us now offer each other the Sign of Peace." The congregation is small enough so that he can leave the altar to shake the hand of everyone present. The Indian people turn shyly to one another, despite the fact that they meet every day. But the familiar ritual is sanctified by the occasion and the presence of the Lord. A tourist is offered a hard hand bound in raised purple veins. The children shake the hands of other children with exaggerated enthusiasm. A little girl's ring comes off during the handshake. She dives to the floor to find it, her starched white dress sticking up like a bobbing duck's tail feathers.

The priest speaks to the individual members of his parish as he shakes each hand.

"Peace be to you, Ed. How's Sarah?"

"Peace be to you, Howard. Did you find that palomino yet?"

"Peace be to you, Nancy. I've got a tourist who's looking for a beaded purse."

"Peace be to you, Al. I hear Howard's having trouble."

At Communion time, every Indian of age rises and heads for the altar. The children start to stampede until firm hands tighten on their shoulders. Then they fall back into their family groups to form a dignified procession.

The priest waits for them before the altar rail. As he places the communion wafer deftly on each tongue, he says: "Body of Christ, Al." "Body of Christ, Nancy." "Body of Christ, Margaret."

When the Mass is over, the people wait for their priest

to walk down the aisle and out the front door. They sing a recessional hymn. Then the people file out, stopping to shake hands with their pastor again on the steps of the church. They mill about on the steps and in the dusty street, talking church business or family business — or just talking.

The sun has climbed higher in the cloudless sky and pours down like molten gold. A few umbrellas are raised, dark mushrooms under which to hide.

For about half an hour the people stand around and visit while the children play noisily. The pastor, still wearing his beaded vestments and now a cowboy hat to protect him from the sun, moves among them, shaking hands ritualistically. Then, when the conversations sputter and die, almost as though on a signal, the people turn and walk their separate ways in the dust.

Just as the prairie brought a new dimension to my concept of space, so the Indian Mass brought a new dimension to my Catholicism. For as human beings are shaped *by* God, so they seek to shape God to their personal or collective needs. Their Christ of the prairies is an Indian Christ, a man of sorrows with a feather in his hair and the pipe of peace in his hands. A Christ who might suddenly appear on the wings of the Thunderbird, as well as on the wings of the dove.

The Christ of the prairies is a waiting Christ, patient as the mountains. A Christ who lives intimately with wind, sand, and stars and the immense solitude of open places. A Christ in patched jeans moving among the poor, the lonely, and the forgotten, breathing into them the breath of hope.

In the total scheme of things, this Sunday morning on a South Dakota Indian reservation may not account for much. Perhaps no more than a grain of sand on the prairie waste. Six white tourists and twenty-two Indians had spent an hour with God. Most of them were poor people, but they left the inheritors of Christ through his sacraments. Most were lonely, but they left with friends. They had touched Christ and their neighbors' hands. Most were quiet people, but they had given their voices in prayer and song.

And the last two lines of one of their hymns seemed to echo:

Hope gently leading me
Nearer, my God, to Thee.

12.

SACRED PLACES

"**A** PLACE WHERE WE SPEAK IN WHISPERS, our words become prayers and our heart falls down and then rises up again."

That was how a ninety-two-year-old Sioux Indian defined a holy place to me. He used the Lakota word *wakaN*, which means holy, sacred, mysterious, and much more. He had led me to a huge, silvery cottonwood on the banks of the Little White River in south-central South Dakota, a place on the Rosebud Sioux Reservation. High in the branches of that tree, which he called *caN wakaN kiN*, the Holy Tree, wrapped in deerskin and bound by leather thongs his infant grandson's remains had been hidden since 1933, thirty-two years before our visit to that spot. And although tree burials were against the white people's law, they were not against the Lakotas'. Probably by now, I thought, the bones had fallen from the tree, to be carried away by the swift current of the river. Or they had been raided by animals. But it was clear to me that the old man beside me saw through the eyes of winters past, believing that the bones of his grandson still hovered above us in the rustling leaves.

"He was to be one of the great ones," he said, his voice husky with emotion, his eyes staring off into some yesterday of the mind, some shining moment of remembrance. "One of the truly great among the Lakotas."

Perhaps so, I thought. We will never know now. Perhaps his grandson would have been the Moses of the Plains Indians, delivering his people from their bondage and leading them to the long promised land. It was good for the old man to think so and God knows the Indians needed all the help they could get in the ways of hope. But the incident and the old man's words have remained in my mind these many years now and I do not think I have ever heard a better definition of a holy place than the one he gave me that bright summer's day.

We all have our holy places, our secret places of remembrance. The public ones, both religious and secular, are well known to us all. Fatima, Lourdes, Medjugorje, Guadalupe. The Statue of Liberty, the Alamo, Omaha Beach, the Vietnam Memorial. Places where we have lost something — or gained something. Perhaps both. We make pilgrimages to those places if we are believers or if we are desperate enough and do not know where or to whom to turn. We look for signs, even miracles to fuel our wavering faiths. We travel with others to these communal places and mix our prayers with theirs. Or perhaps we only watch with them, watch and hope, our disbelief the burden that we would lay down along with our crutches, our wheelchairs. In public we act as others act. But in the secret grottos of our hearts....

I remember another definition of a holy place. It was spoken by a mother who had gone on a long-delayed pilgrimage to a faraway military cemetery to visit her son's grave. The journey had been a great sacrifice to her, both financially and emotionally. A journey that hurt. And finally she stood on a lonely ridge and prayerfully surveyed the scene. With its row after row of crosses and stars it looked like a geometric garden of death waiting for the harvest. The harvest of resurrection perhaps. The stark simplicity of the markers made the fields more tragic than Gothic spires or ornate monuments might have. For it frequently happens that the most powerful symbols of sorrow are the plainest.

"I don't think I'll look for his place alone," she said in a frail voice, yet strangely, one filled with renewed hope. "They're so much alike this way I'll just think of them all as my sons." After all the years! After all the miles! After all the anticipation of this moment she had surrendered her private sorrow for a greater sorrow. And perhaps there is no greater love than that — feeling another's pain as one's own. Adopting another's dead.

But most definitions of sacred places are made in the heart's silence, without benefit of words. And sometimes without benefit of reason, logic, or other special proclamation. It may be a place of happiness as well as sorrow or it may be a place where joy and sorrow are mixed in the proportion we call "bittersweet."

I knew a man who, for years after the death of his wife, returned to a place in the Catskill Mountains, the place where they had first met and where they had spent their honeymoon. I knew him well enough to ask: Doesn't it get you down going there now — and alone.

He gave me a look, a ye-of-little-faith look, and smiled tolerantly. "No," he answered, "I am happier there than anywhere else on earth precisely because I am no longer alone."

And in that moment I could tell that I still saw through a glass darkly. With the help of some others I have come to understand.

For over the years I too have had my special places and sentimental journeys. The town where I grew up,

made most of my memories, and finally left for war.
The place where I planted a maple tree in memory of
a boy who was growing into a man, a place where I was
afraid to return lest the boy be gone forever. The movie
theater that was my launching pad into other worlds,
worlds of the imagination. I think the writer that I became was born there — on those ripped and worn seats
in the magical dark. A church where I first knew God, a
church that has been long since demolished for a newer
church. And the shrine out back — gone too! A place on
the white sands of the New Mexican desert where the
human-made sun exploded one day and fused the sands
into a hard rock of lost innocence, a solid tear for what
had been and what would never be again. The mass
grave at Wounded Knee that holds the bones of Chief
Big Foot's band and the lost and trampled dreams of a
people.

But a special place is not a sacred place just as a journey is not a pilgrimage. There is a difference. A sacred
place is not a place of memory alone: it is a place of
felt experience, a place where the past and present come
together to make a new moment, a richer moment —
perhaps a revelation or even an epiphany.

I did not learn these things until a friend said something that stuck in my mind and became for me a truth
to live by, said something that drew together an old Indian's words and the words of a Gold Star mother into
a welding of truth.

He told me he was going back to Europe for the first
time since World War II. Now that he was sixty-five he
had some unfinished business to attend to and it was
getting late. He was going to visit a memorial for American airmen who were killed in the war. He was going
to visit a little chapel that had been the scene of his rec-
onciliation with God. Still a flier, he was going to rent a

plane and fly through the scenes of those air battles that
still came to him in the stillness of the night. He was going to visit the places he had bombed and perhaps ask
someone, some survivor for forgiveness.

When he told me his plans I stared at him in disbelief. Certainly he knew as I did that the cities had risen,
Phoenix-like from the ashes we had all helped to make.
Many had been rebuilt into something grander, something more splendid than what had stood before. The
only ruins now were the human ruins — the survivors of
the firestorms, their faces burned smooth as satin masks.
The dull, animal eyes that rose with every thunderclap,
every unknown sound from above. The old who had
never been young.

And the scenes of aerial battles — they too were gone,
wiped clean as a child's slate by time and weather. For
the skies are ever-changing, ever-shifting: the greatest
air battles in all history had left no more trace than
yesterday's thunderstorm or a child's balloon lost. The
contrails; the men and machines; the angry sky filled
with flak; the parachutes; the smell of burning fuel; the
bombs exploding — gone, all gone! On the ground there
are remains — graves, memorials. There are rusting
tanks, unexploded bombs, and craters. There are pock-
marked walls where people, sometimes whole villages
faced machine guns, and there are the terrible furnaces
of death. There are clues, bits of evidence at least that
millions of people died. But the skies? Even over Hi-
roshima they clear to forgetfulness and the sun emerges
to shine on flowers as well as the human images burned
in stone.

And so I asked my friend what it was he was going
to see — with the cities rebuilt and the sky cleared and
new generations walking the streets? It would be even
crueler perhaps with so many memories gone. So many

things forgotten. What was there to see after so long a time? What remained?

For a moment he looked at me, surprised. Then he said the words that I have never forgotten: "What makes it sacred is what you bring to it, you know. The sacredness — that's inside us."

REMEMBRANCE

The minstrel tears of memory shed their songs
On cloven stone where the single flower grows
Lightward from its narrow cell of shade
Beyond the reach of noon. The requiem of wind flows
Like a spoken river over the bed of yesterdays,
Mosaic in its thirst. It is a miracle of bloom,
Nourished by a lonely night or a scale of laughter
In the way that footsteps fill an empty room.

13.

REFLECTIONS ON A CATHOLIC BOYHOOD

As A BOY I DIDN'T DREAM that my hometown would some day creep toward the city, dragging a carpet of blacktop and concrete behind it. In those days, I could still see cornstalks nodding in the sun and hear the night trains pulling into the station. Sometimes I could even see a team of oxen plodding along as their gravel-voiced owner cursed them through the streets. And once or twice a year, a Gypsy caravan would rattle through town looking for scissors and knives to sharpen, and children to steal away, my Irish grandmother warned me.

Now, looking back, I often blame the Helderberg Mountains to the west: they gave me a false sense of permanence, as though they and everything else were eternal. I didn't know that time could pass over mountains, too, like a wearing wind. At other times I blame my innocent imagination that built a wall around what I wanted to protect from change. Only much later did I recognize that fifth column that many people call progress.

In those days, you could fire buckshot into any holiday crowd and not be likely to hit a Catholic. My hometown was largely white, Protestant, and Republican. The few Catholics were mostly Irish or Italian, and Democratic. And most lived on the wrong side of the railroad tracks, the old American boundary which sliced small towns in half. The houses that trembled to the thud of freight cars were Catholic, and crucifixes danced on the walls and plaster saints stumbled to the edges of tables whenever a train went through.

The postmaster of our town was Catholic and Democratic, for those were the early days of President Franklin D. Roosevelt and the New Deal. The two barbers who shared a shop were Italian Catholics. The railroad men, mostly Irish, were Catholics. I remember seeing them in their shapeless overalls, keeping the strange hours of men who stormed the night on a head of steam and a whistle. A good number of the pale, starched clerks who worked in the state office buildings were Catholics, and so were most of the ragged old ladies who cleaned those buildings by night. The small force of anonymous laborers who carried lunch pails into the gray morning were Catholics. The tavern owner was a Catholic. So was the dapper bookmaker who put a neatly creased $5 bill in the collection basket every Sunday, causing us younger boys to ponder the wages of sin. There were others, too, some on the perimeter of prominence, but most Catholics were simply working people. The leaders of the community — political, professional, business, and social — were all non-Catholics, and many were anti-Catholics.

There is no denying that there was much prejudice, even discrimination, against Catholics then; no overt hostility, but a subtle, guarded discrimination that was never mentioned in places of influence and power. There was just quiet exclusion, casual neglect. Even then I sensed that the situation was perpetuated by ignorance and irrational fear. Ignorance of what Catholics believed and how they lived, and fear of the unknown.

So much of Roman Catholicism was mysterious then, shrouded in the dark corridors of the past and the musty catacombs of dimly remembered evils. Gregorian chants and the heavy tolling of bells called up images of hooded monks in procession toward yesterday. The Catholics, it was whispered, had sworn allegiance to a foreign power, perhaps in blood. Everything the pope touched turned to gold while good people starved. Mass, of course, was said in Latin, as solemn and mysterious to my neighbors as the sounds of Roman legions in the night. The confessionals, tiny Gothic cubicles tucked away in dark corners beneath plaster saints, heard secret sins whispered from the deepest corners of the self. And there was the rosary, those mysterious beads told over and over again.

It all sounds a bit silly now that we have college courses in comparative religion and television programs about mixed marriages. The ethnic comedians now make jokes about old mysteries. But when there was laughter in those days, it was nervous laughter, just an octave below a scream.

But even prejudice can have some good effects. One was that the Catholic minority joined together in a camaraderie I have not known since, a kind of spiritual underground.

You would go to the Italian barber in town rather than to a more fashionable shop in the city because he played the organ at Mass or because his wife decorated the altar with flowers she had grown herself. You felt close to them because they shared your most vital experiences with God. You knelt beside them. You followed them around the church, making the Stations of the Cross. You went to the Catholic grocer, even though the A & P prices were lower, because he taught the catechism to children on Saturday afternoons. You might not have traveled in the same circles, but when you met another Catholic on the street, something passed between you, perhaps a recognition that this man, too, waited in the dark for the healing words of absolution. Or abstained from meat on Fridays. Or quoted by heart the same prayers you did. Or shared with you the Body and Blood of Christ. And if you were a young lad, you called him *Mister*, and stopped to ask about his wife or children or his business. That spirit had nothing to do with tokenism, fear, or legal obligation. It was a kind of grassroots democratic urge, springing from a felt spiritual kinship. It even extended to those who were handicapped physically, mentally, or emotionally.

Every Catholic parish in those days seemed to have its Holy Fool, a mentally handicapped man or boy who haunted the church grounds, and sometimes worked there. I don't see them anymore, the ones shoveling snow or cutting grass or weeding flowers or plastering over a crack in a wall. Perhaps they have been institutionalized in the name of charity and now sit on empty benches and watch the flowers they once tended.

I remember one altar boy named Flann. He had a tumble of straw-colored hair that looked as though it had been turned by a pitchfork. His eyes were dull, staring off into some yesterday of the mind. His voice was deep, and he had a habit of swallowing his words, especially the Latin responses he had memorized but which held no meaning for him except that, in some strange way, they served the Lord.

I remember Flann's finest hour. One old lady in a black shawl had shuffled to the altar railing for Communion and, because she knelt in the darkness by the Christmas crèche, she was not noticed by the priest. But Flann saw her, and stood by her like a faithful dog. The priest returned to the altar, prepared to continue with the Mass, but Flann did not follow him. He stood fast, the paten poised beneath the old woman's quivering chin. Seconds that seemed like hours passed. The priest looked around for Flann and finally saw him, standing there at attention. The priest, realizing his oversight, took up the ciborium again and hurried back. The ghost of a smile crossed Flann's face as the host was lowered to the old woman's tongue. The priest, too, smiled his apology and returned to the altar. The old woman made the Sign of the Cross and waited for the tabernacle door to close, then she struggled to her feet and moved silently back to her pew.

It wasn't much of an incident in the dramatic history of the church. But an old woman had been spared some humiliation. And a mentally handicapped altar boy had served the Lord in the only way he knew, by waiting. I have long ago forgotten the boundaries of the Holy Roman Empire but I don't believe I shall ever forget Flann's wait upon the Lord. It has stuck in some corner of my memory for thirty years.

There were those who were physically deformed, too. One was Monk, a hunchback who carried his early sorrow like a pack on his back. As a boy I thought of it as a saint's baggage. And years later, I tried to express the idea in a poem:

The sole survivor of himself,
He crawls from his tunnel's dark
Into another Sunday, belled as any upright hymn.
Even Cain bore no such mark,
Set heavier for innocence
Upon the living mountain of his days.
Slowly, he tolls himself to light a candle,
Warms his straightened memory in a blaze

That spits back the sullen moment like a curse.
The congregation ebbs, feels free
To cast him saint, sinner, jester, scapegoat —
As mythologies decree.
At communion he remains the scavenger of prayer
While his altar-ego soars free,
Perfectly misshapen, to share his sad Redeemer
With those who only see.

There were others, too, like Henry, a gaunt blade of a man who directed the choir between bouts of drinking. He lived alone in a huge, gray house with stained-glass windows that perhaps colored his loneliness. He spoke Latin like a Roman orator, and the hymns he directed broke from the choir loft like great waves and washed over the congregation. Nobody really knew why he drank so much, but his penance was done in song.

It seemed that, in those days, every parish had its Henrys, Monks, or Flanns — characters, I thought as a boy, who had been singled out by God to tell us something of ourselves. To me they were living parables to tell us of compassion, tolerance, and the strange, holy beauty of the grotesque. Yes, and even to teach us wisdom.

The old, red brick Church of Saint Thomas is gone now. On the spot where it stood is the blacktop parking lot of a new church that seems to have risen from the ashes of memory. It is almost as though the old structure had taken a direct hit from a powerful bomb. The shrine of the Virgin that stood in back of the old church has been moved across the street to a place in front of the new elementary school. Next to the new church is a rectory in matching stone, complete with modern offices and living quarters.

My hometown isn't by any means predominantly

Catholic today, but the odds on hitting a Catholic in a holiday crowd are much better.

Old Father H., who looked like a bald Barry Fitzgerald and attended to everything himself, in his nervous Irish way, has been replaced by a monsignor and three assistants. We have lay teachers, secretaries, and professional groundskeepers. The church-school complex is run with computerized efficiency. The Masses start on time. The congregation doesn't have to wait while Father H. hurries back from an all-night sick call to offer the six o'clock Mass. Or while Flann wrestles into his cassock and surplice or searches for a burned-out fuse. Or while Henry has a last cup of black coffee before leaving his lonely, gray house for a Sunday morning burst of song.

14.

JUGGLERS, BELL RINGERS, EXILES

THEY WERE LIKE THE FIFTEENTH STATION of the Cross, so much were the mentally handicapped and emotionally ill a part of the parish in those days. The mentally handicapped altar boys like Flann, those "fools for Christ." Or the hunchback, Monk, whose physical deformity drove him into the dark corners. Or Henry, whose mind was dulled by alcohol and seemed only to come alive on the swells of music from his choir loft. But they were all accepted and often served the parish and their Lord in mysterious ways, reminding us almost daily that there but for the grace of God go each of us.

This was back in the '30s and early '40s, before the ones we now identify as "handicapped" or "emotionally disturbed" were sent off to special schools, sometimes to state institutions. In those days people were less inclined to diagnose and treat forms of mental handicap, they couldn't afford special care, and there weren't many agencies that dealt with such problems. So it was up to family, relatives, and friends. And the greater parish community.

The mentally handicapped were a part of our lives then, and sometimes we all learned from them about sacrifice, devotion, and the unique insights they had to offer. . . .

I remember an old man named Pedro, a Mexican-American who lived alone on the New Mexico desert in an adobe house his father had left him. Early on the morning of July 16, 1945, he saw what he thought was the end of the world, an explosion so awesome and intensely brilliant that a frightened blind girl miles beyond hearing had asked her mother: "What was that?"

For an instant her darkness had been made visible. A miracle of sorts, an unholy one.

Although Pedro had not always been a faithful parishioner over the years, he hurried to the priest like Chicken Little with the news that the sky was falling. For he had seen the horizon lit by the light of many suns. He had seen a cloud of fire climb miles into the sky, turning from ball to mushroom shape as it rose.

Patiently, the priest tried to explain the happening as he had heard it explained on the radio. A military test. Somewhere near Alamogordo on the desert. After all, there was still a war on.

But Pedro wasn't satisfied. Hadn't the earth moved beneath his feet? Hadn't a thousand noons lit the early morning? Wasn't that what the Lord said would happen? And in his hand he still clutched a piece of bluish-green jade fused by the sand and heat: he held it like a holy relic, for it had rained from the sky, the tangible proof of a terrible vision.

Because he thought the end was near he insisted that

the priest hear his confession, and even tried to get him to bless the "holy stone."

And that was the only time in his long life that Pedro ever confused the work of human beings with the work of God.

He returned to the church and did its humbler work with a passion. He carved a new Seventh Station; the old one had been broken by a painter's falling ladder. He kept the flowers alive on the graves behind the church. He plastered cracks in the walls. He rang the bells by hand, jerking to their vibrating music like a puppet on a string. He brought food and clothing to the poor. He went to Communion at every opportunity. He worked like a lesser apostle and waited for eternity. And when it came he was clutching his ikon of blasted sand as though it were the key to the kingdom.

I remember a Sioux Indian boy named Joe who lived on one of the reservations in South Dakota, a boy who had been "lightning struck" when he was very young. Some said he had been touched by *Wakinyan*, the Thunder Beings, and had great power. Others said he was *witko*, which not only means "crazy" in the Lakota language but "sacred" and "holy" as well.

As he grew older he was drawn to the church like a magnet to the north. He was attracted mostly by the colorful mysteries and their symbols — dark confessionals, the stained-glass saints, and the burning altar light. What he didn't understand he accepted on faith.

His parish was dirt poor and his church sat on top of a hill that rose like a tidal wave from a sea of grass. When it rained hard there was flash-flooding and the gravel roads washed out or turned to mud. Only the horses could make it through; the old cars and pickups didn't even try. Sometimes there were fewer than ten people at a rainy Sunday's Mass. More than once it was just the priest and Joe, riding bareback through the mud and rain like circuit preachers in earlier times. Together they said Mass to liturgical echoes.

Joe did most of the work around the church, the routine maintenance that winter blizzards and summer heat and storms made necessary. He became a carpenter, painter, mason. He worked with everything but electricity, whose arching bluish flame still reminded him of a day when darkness came at noon and the Thunder Beings spoke in tongues of fire. Joe wouldn't even change a light bulb.

Joe was an artist as well as craftsman. He carved an Indian Christ hanging from a cross and the priest hung it over the tabernacle for all to see. He painted Thunderbirds and crossed Sacred Pipes in bright pastels, colors that gave the old church an Easter look. Working like a prairie Michelangelo, on his back, balanced on a board between two ladders, he even painted a giant Thunderbird ringed by angels on the ceiling.

Some members of the congregation complained to the priest about the native look the church was getting. The bishop, descending in a whirling of dust and thumping helicopter blades, called it "interesting." Some angry churchgoers even transferred to other parishes.

But the Indian people responded to Joe's efforts and within a year church membership had doubled. Scholars and tourists came to stare, admire, and take pictures. A newspaperman from Rapid City did a story on the Indian church. And there was an article in a national Catholic magazine.

There were converts, too, and a return of lapsed Catholics, won over by Joe's inner vision that wedded the symbols of a native tradition and a more orthodox Christianity. In one small prairie parish, the Great Spirit and Christ had become one.

Once Joe saved the church and his work from a raging prairie fire. While others were fleeing or carrying out the things that might be saved, Joe stood before the inferno and challenged it, shouting to the Four Directions and Jesus to spare the church. He hurled a garbled prayer into the smoke and flames, drawing closer by the moment, and then a minor miracle took place: the winds turned around and the fire died, feeding on its ashes.

I don't know what happened to Joe. The last time I was on the reservation someone told me he had gone to live with his sister in Denver. Another said he was in an institution in Omaha — or was it Sioux Falls? No matter. It was far from the prairie church he had saved and given back to his people.

But I found that Joe was remembered in a curious way. For now and then some of the older Indians refer to their church on the hill not by its official name, but as St. Joseph's.

And then there was Mike.

In his story there is no high drama; no A-bombs or lightning bolts. He was just an altar boy content to remain a boy while others grew to troubled manhood.

Mike served his old Irish priest and friend at every Mass. He had trouble with language, even the English language, but his Latin responses would have done credit to a classical scholar. The words had no meaning for him; they were sounds he had memorized, but they rang through St. Thomas Church like bits of oratory from the Roman senate.

For seventeen years Mike served the church, its pastor, and its people. He built the shrine to Mary at the rear of the church and he tended the flowers planted there. He was there when children made their First Communions and later when they were confirmed, married, and even buried. If the old priest was the heart of St. Thomas parish, then Mike was its pulse.

Then the pastor died suddenly of a massive stroke. The bishop celebrated the Requiem Mass, assisted by five or six priests who had been friends. Mike, by then in his late twenties, sat on the altar with the celebrants but he took no part. He just sat there, shoulders hunched, bent forward like a priest at the consecration. And when he looked into the open casket, a crucifixion was in his face.

I don't know what Mike saw in the satin-lined coffin or what went through his mind. But he left town soon after, hopped a freight in the middle of the night. And no one has ever heard from him.

If Mike survived the death of his world he would be close to sixty now. I like to think he *did* survive and that he found a home in some other parish and that he also has found the God behind the man of flesh and blood that he so loved and served.

Last Sunday I attended a Latin Mass, the first since those old days at St. Thomas. It wasn't the same somehow. When the priest pronounced the solemn phrases there were no loyal echoes, except from the past.

Pedro, Joe, and Mike. They are not isolated cases. They have been a part of the church since the beginning, in fact and fiction: the hunchback of Notre Dame, the juggler at the shrine of the Virgin, the bell ringer — perhaps even Simon the Cyrenian who helped an anguished Lord carry his cross. For according to Matthew: " . . . they brought unto Him all the sick people that were taken with diverse diseases and torments." And maybe they still do.

In my present parish there is a man-child who sits quietly in his pew during most of the Mass. But when the priest announces: "Let us offer one another a sign of peace," he comes to life, springs to his feet and shakes hands warmly with everyone within ten rows. He greets each one like a prodigal son returned and seems to make a public offering of his flesh.

Look closely in your own parish. They are there — but not among the highly visible. You won't find them on the altar giving the scriptural readings. You won't find them distributing Communion, or acting as ushers. They won't be among those on the parish council or the school board. But look at the one who unexpectedly shakes your hand on the sidewalk after Mass.

Look at the jugglers, the bell ringers, all those fragile exiles who serve the Lord so humbly and so faithfully. Perhaps the Lord himself should have the final word on them all: *Unless ye become as little children, ye shall not enter the Kingdom of Heaven.*

15.

THE UNBELIEVER
IN MY CHURCH

I HAVE A FRIEND WHO GOES TO MASS every Sunday, every Holy Day — yet he doesn't believe in God. He wasn't baptized a Catholic. His only ties with the church are emotional. My friend is a good neighbor in the Christian sense. He has a good mind, a challenging job, and a loving family. As he approaches the far side of middle age he is successful, as the world measures success. He seems to have everything — everything but God.

Before I knew him well, I assumed he was a believer. I was surprised by the fact that he never received the sacraments, but I supposed that, eventually, he would receive them. He may have had his own good reasons, I told myself. But one morning over coffee he told me the truth.

I was stunned by his confession. I broke the heavy silence that followed with what I thought was the logical question: "Then why do you go to Mass so faithfully?"

"It is the *idea* of God that I love," he told me. "And I love the things that support it — the church, its architecture, art, music, the liturgy, the stories. I love it all. In a time when everything seems secular and transient...." He stopped himself, sighed, and then summed up: "Those things represent the finest expression of our greatest hope."

I noticed a sadness in his voice, the sadness of a child who has put away childish things but is not yet a man.

"Hopes come true sometimes," I reminded him, but he just looked away as if from a strong light.

I tried again. I asked him if it wouldn't be better if his love could be returned. It seemed like such a bargain, I told him, a divine love for a human one.

He half smiled. "The things you love — they don't have to love you back, you know."

I looked hard at my friend bent over his coffee. At that moment he seemed beyond me and my influence — a kind of existential hero, the lonely, isolated man who neither believes nor is happy in his unbelief. He was a man as remote as a character in fiction.

In a moment he looked up and went on. He said he loved the drama of the Mass and the music that accompanied it. He loved the quiet look of alabaster saints, stained-glass windows, the Stations of the Cross. He loved the ballet of spitting candles in the semi-darkness. He loved the glorious sweep of cathedrals in distant cities. He loved the dark confessionals where sins were unloaded for absolution. He loved the prayers, responses, Gospels, and the lives of the saints.

I remained the good listener. I nodded, knowing that most Catholics loved those things, too — ceremony, history, symbol, and ritual. We had been brought up with them. They were all a part of our faith, an important part. But what did they mean without God?

My friend's confession ended with pain and vagueness. "Well, sometime maybe — " And that was all. He drained his cup and swallowed what for me might have been the real mystery.

At Communion time, when others approach the altar to receive Him, my friend remains in place, a look of pain and longing on his face. Almost a look of jealousy. He sits apart like one of the lepers in the Gospels, ringing a silent bell and peeking through a hole in the wall at the celebration inside. Forever on the outside looking in. His disease is not leprosy but a debilitating reason: He cannot make the leap over the wall, the leap to faith.

My friend is certainly not alone in his inability to believe. It is a symptom of a modern *malaise*, if not the disease itself. Yet most unbelievers do not haunt the places where others worship. They affect a scorn or an indifference for such places. They go their separate, secular ways.

I cannot presume to know the secret warrings of my friend's heart, the darker nights of his soul. And I can only guess at the still-born prayers, the fierce hunger to believe. No one can fathom the depths of another's yearning. It is almost a sin to try. But if it is true that "the way to heaven is through hell" then he may be on the first leg of that journey, wearily counting the milestones toward a destination unknown.

More than twenty years have passed since that coffee conversation. My friend still goes to Mass alone. Sundays, Holy Days, Ash Wednesday, All Souls Days — he is there. But he still refuses to join the Lord's banquet. A generation of priests and well-meaning friends have tried to convert him. But to what? You cannot put on faith like an overcoat, without believing. My friend is too honest for that. And so he waits.

One day not long ago I entered what I thought was an empty church to ask a favor of God. The day was so cloudy and dark that the stained-glass windows were like photographic negatives. When my eyes finally adjusted to the dim light I was surprised to see my friend up near the front of the church. He was staring at the huge crucifix that dominated the space above the altar. Minutes later I saw that his lips were moving.

I made my petition quickly and left, almost as though I had been an intruder on some secret and sacred rite.

I like to think that one day God will reach out and touch my friend, saying something like: "Arise and walk with Me." Touch him, perhaps, as he kneels in an empty church. I like to think that faith will finally come to him like dawn to the desert, blood-red and hymning praise. But that may be a scenario for fiction rather than providence. Meanwhile I shall go on praying for him, and at the same time wondering whether my own belief has come too easily. Have I been denied some rewarding struggle that makes salvation sweeter?

As I grow older I know fewer answers. But I do know that my friend is a seeker. He may be looking for something I have found without recognizing it, some precious ore of meaning that I stumbled over and do not even now know the value of.

It doesn't matter so much how one comes to God. Loving the *idea* of God may lead to talking with God in a silent church, just as loneliness may lead to talking with oneself. Loving the words of prayer may lead to believing those words. It's a good beginning, loving is.

16.

A THURSDAY'S PASSION

Sт. JOHN'S Roman Catholic Church dominates a shabby block of Temple Street in Worcester, Massachusetts, about halfway between Springfield and Boston. Its white spire seems to rise like a phoenix from the ash-gray ugliness of the surrounding neighborhood. It is an old and delicate church, but you get the impression it is one of the survivors, that it will be around for a long time and that even urban renewal will have to tiptoe carefully around it. You get the feeling that St. John's is something special, really *special*. And it is. For in a few hour's time it will explode in a Thursday's passion!

Thursday at noon is when the Charismatic Renewal Movement service is scheduled to begin, but the crowds start arriving at daybreak. A few have been there all night. None of the believers calls the service by such a pretentious name: to them it is simply the healing service of Father DiOrio.

The crowds come by plane, car, chartered bus, and wheelchair. Catholic and non-Catholic, doubter and believer. They come from a few blocks away and they come from Australia; from nearby Boston and Bonn, Ger-

many — the curious, the desperate, the deformed, the
sick, the dying. They come with hope to this Lourdes
on a one-way street. No one has to look closely at the
sign to know that Temple Street is one-way: the parade
of broken bodies that travel it is proof enough.

Inside, in a church designed for a few thousand there
are close to ten thousand. They huddle in the basement,
hang from the balconies, fill the vestibule, and spill out
into the street. It is standing room only — as usual.
Crutches, walkers, wheelchairs, and the other machinery
of pain are in evidence everywhere. There is confusion.
A blind man stumbles to find his seat. A mentally handicapped child chants a separate, sing-song liturgy above
the piano music that comes from the altar. The air is elec-
tric with hope and expectation. The stakes are high —
bodies, minds, souls. The undercurrent of hushed voices
rises and falls in a low tide of sound.

Quite suddenly the mixed congregation of regular
parishioners and visitors picks up a tune from the piano
player and breaks into song. There is no signal from
anyone. It just *happens* — like so much else at Father
DiOrio's service. It begins with a few tentative voices
and swells until it fills the packed church. The tunes
are well known though some like "You'll Never Walk
Alone" are not usually associated with Catholic services.
Others are more traditional: "Were You There?" and
"How Great Thou Art." The people sway hypnotically
as they sing, holding out their raised hands, palms up,
as though to sift the sound of their own voices before
sending them to God.

Halfway down the center aisle there is a large, wo-
ven basket on a table. Called the "petition basket," it is
overflowing with scraps of paper written by those with
special intentions for healing — physical, mental, emotional, or spiritual. A basket of hope, a basket of word

prayers, many scrawled in pain. Seed for a harvest of faith.

There are elements of showmanship in the preparations for the service. The atmosphere is theatrical in some ways. The piano has been joined by three guitars, each with its separate microphone. The lights dim, allowing the row of altar candles to dance brightly in their red holders. People are buying souvenirs in the vestibule. The altar cloth is a brilliant red. So too are the jackets of the many ushers who patrol the aisles attempting to control the overflow crowd. Between hymns the concerted hum of voices is like the anxious buzzing of a Broadway audience just before the curtain rises.

But high drama has always been a part of religious ceremony. Drama was born of a *spiritual* hunger....

Father Ralph DiOrio has the battered face of a professional fighter and the heavy, sensitive eyes of a poet. He has served the Lord on the streets of Chicago and among the Indians in Canada. He has been in the combat zones of faith; he has seen it all. Dressed in a black cassock and carrying a crucifix he appears on the altar to welcome the congregation. The people respond perceptibly to his presence: there is a current, a communication that passes between the priest and his ministry, a secret sharing. Like many with strong faces he has a gentle voice, a gentle manner. His hands fly gracefully as he speaks, tracing a language of their own on the heavy air.

He announces the theme of this Thursday's service, "The Wounds of Christ," and proceeds to deliver a five-minute homily on the subject. His words come easily, informally, as though he were speaking to a few individuals rather than to the thousands gathered. His talk is even laced with humor and gentle satire at times. When he finishes his message he asks the crowd to praise the

Lord with him. Dividing the congregations into equal sections with a slicing motion of his hand he asks them to sing the note struck by a voice on one of the microphones behind him. Different notes for the four sections, a sort of spiritual round. In response to his appeal the humming swells until it is like something about to explode. A testing of the engines of faith before taking off.

While the notes surge with the power of a distant dynamo, Father DiOrio roams the aisles in a random search for those who need him. He approaches a woman who appears to be in her seventies, a woman who has not spoken in years according to the testimony of her sister beside her.

"Pray with me," the priest whispers into the microphone around his neck.

He reaches out to lay his hands on the woman but she crumples like a rag doll and is eased to the floor by gentle hands. Her eyes are closed, her hands folded across her breast, and the ghost of a smile plays on her face. When she is raised from her swoon of a few minutes she cries out in a clear, metallic voice: "Praise the Lord!"

Then she breaks down at the sound of her own voice and begins to sob while her sister screams hysterically. The congregation gasps, almost as a single person, and breaks into spontaneous cheering and applause.

Above the swell of voices still holding on to a musical note as though to life itself, the calmer voice of Father DiOrio is heard praising the Lord. Those closest to him move nearer, attempting to touch him but he waves them off.

"It isn't necessary to touch me," he tells them. "I am not the one responsible. It is the work of the Holy Spirit. I am only the channel of God. His instrument. Your praise should be for Jesus."

He moves up the aisle and stops beside a woman supported by metal crutches.

"God has brought me to this woman," he says. "God works in mysterious and random ways.   Pray with me."

He touches the woman and she slumps to one side where arms hold her and ease her into the seat.

The priest stands in the aisle waiting, his hands outstretched, his eyes closed in prayer. When the woman revives he speaks to her.

"Walk to me," he orders gently.

The woman begins to cry.

"I can't do it, Father. I haven't walked without my crutches in years."

"Walk with me," he urges.

The woman moves her crutches aside, grips the back of the pew in front of her and pulls herself to her feet. Tears stream from her eyes and her lips move in silent prayer.

"Don't be afraid," the priest says quietly. "The Holy Spirit is with you. You are not alone. The Holy Spirit is pushing you toward me — "

The woman moves to the aisle.

"Let go of the pew and walk to me."

A few side steps, a shuffle, and she is in the aisle.

"Do you feel any pain?"

She shakes her head and takes a baby step. The priest backs away and holds out his hands.   The chorus of voices rises in expectation, in support, until it becomes a human prayer-swell.

The woman takes another step. Another. The fear seems to pass from her face. The agony. The doubt. In a moment she is shuffling down the aisle toward the priest. He takes her hand, and while the crowd applauds wildly they walk to the altar. Then, smiling, she walks alone back to her seat, nodding timidly at the supportive crowd.

Father DiOrio moves on, speaking quietly into his microphone. Fragments of Latin, Spanish, Italian. Speaking in tongues.

A woman wearing a neck brace steps into the aisle. He touches her and she collapses like a puppet on a broken string. The priest turns from her to a deaf man.

In a few minutes there are ten bodies on the floor of St. John's stretched out like a child's abandoned toys. Some people keel over as the priest passes. He comes back to each of the fallen, sometimes to kneel over them in prayer. The woman in the neck brace rises and with the help of a nun removes her brace. Then she bends over and touches her toes at the priest's command. The man who was deaf, his voice husky and unsynchronized, speaks a garbled tongue at first. But in less than five minutes everyone in the church is able to understand him.

Father DiOrio turns to the balcony.

"Three women came here today with lumps in their breasts. You know who you are. If you will examine yourselves you will find that the lumps have disappeared."

There is a pause, then a silence that is finally shattered by screams of astonishment and relief....

And so it goes on. For three hours the healing continues. Emotions have peaked and subsided a hundred or more times. It seems impossible to sustain the intensity of the first hour of the service. But it happens. The temperature inside the church has risen twenty degrees at least. Coats are shed, neckties and scarfs loosened. The people are quieter now, but it is the quiet of stunned reverence, the quiet of emotions drained. The quiet of peace.

The crowds still swarm to touch the priest but he rejects them gently, protesting that it has not been his work but the work of the Holy Spirit.

"I am only the channel," he says again and again. "The channel of God. Only His instrument. I have no power apart from Him. Praise Jesus!"

He asks the people to offer each other the Sign of Peace. Some shake hands but in the lingering ecstasy most embrace. Some weep openly now that the tension is over and they can touch the frailty of flesh — flesh that has been mended and healed in different ways.

Father DiOrio reminds them again: "Some healing of the Holy Spirit you have witnessed. But there is other healing that is taking place now. And some will continue to take place after you have left St. John's.

"I want you to think of someone who has wronged or injured you. Perhaps as far back as your childhood even. I want you to think of them and forgive them as God has forgiven you."

After it is over there is the Eucharist. It is the *real* climax to the service for there are those *walking* to the altar to receive the host who came on crutches or in wheelchairs. There are those hearing the words, "Body of Christ" for the first time. Those answering "Amen" for the first time. Those kneeling....

The service I witnessed that Thursday was Father DiOrio's first at St. John's in a month. He had just returned from Duluth, Minnesota, where he had conducted similar teaching and healing seminars. The crowds in his home parish seemed to hunger for his return.

Father DiOrio's healings, though he takes no credit for them, have included practically everything from cancer to sinus. Physicians have written testimony that some of the things that happen at the services have no medical explanation. Individual cases have been investigated, documented, and authenticated. But as one might expect in the rarer atmosphere of faith, there is controversy and debate. Undoubtedly it will go on for a long time to come. Meanwhile at St. John's there are cripples walking, deaf people hearing....

I asked a friend, a priest who was familiar with the work of Father DiOrio, what he thought about it all. But he didn't take the bait; he didn't want to be drawn into a discussion.

"There is plenty of precedent," he said vaguely. "In the life of Christ and in the church. If people are better off...."

Like plenty of others including my priest friend, I am predominantly a "head" Catholic. A doubting Thomas, not fully believing and yet not happy in my disbelief. But like many of us in this time and place I am a *seeker* too.

I have looked for the Messiah reborn at Wounded Knee. I have looked with Noah Jumping Eagle for the Lord in the V of a cottonwood tree. Looked for the Dark Virgin of Guadalupe on a mountaintop in New Mexico. I have looked with old Elijah into the life-blood of his people's songs. Looked with Father Benitez for the ghosts of Sundays past. Looked with the *Yuwipi Wicasa* for the spirits that come on the wings of faith in darkened rooms. I have looked and prayed with holy men and women on the plains and in the desert. And at rare times I have even looked inside myself. And each looking, each prayer has been one of the Stations of my stumbling journey....

I don't know what drew me to St. John's in Worcester on a rainy March day. A city I had never seen before. It wasn't pain or illness, thank God. It wasn't desperation or despair. I don't think it had to do with destiny or even *deja vu*. But maybe I am looking too deeply....

Maybe it was really simple. I was a writer and there

was a human drama going on there. Or maybe like the publican Zaccheus in Luke's Gospel I discovered once again that I was too short to see clearly and had to climb a tree....

DATE DUE

HIGHSMITH   # 45220